表紙イラスト

　Unity Architecture は人や物、自然との間に働く因果律の全体の輪郭を示しています。

　本書では、その始まりを中心の下部構造と上部構造を横断するフィンランドのナショナル・ロマンティシズムに見出しています。その矢印に角度を与えることで、ナショナル・ロマンティシズムを第三の場所に適用できるネーション・オブ・ソロウとし、その回転運動の軌跡が「あるデザインのフィールド」を形成します。その輪郭をクロスオーバー・アーキテクチュアとシナスタジア・シーナリーの考えが互いに引っ張り合うことでできた Learning from Finlandia というフィールドに、3 つのクロスオーバー・プロジェクトが成り立っています。

The Cover Art

　Unity Architecture outlines the whole causality that works between people, things and nature.

　In this book, its beginning is found in Finnish National Romanticism, which crosses over the centre line dividing the substructure and superstructure. By giving an angle to the arrow, National Romanticism becomes Nation of Sorrow that makes it apply to a third place, and the trajectory of its rotational movement forms "A Field of Designs". That trajectory is stretched by the idea of Crossover-Architecture and Synesthesia Scenery and expanded to make the field of Learning from Finlandia. Three Xover Projects are established on the field.

3 Projects,

3 Exhibitions,

Unity **18** Objects
Architecture

Edited & Written by

Taishi WATANABE

本書の構成
Structure of this book

　本書は異なる都市で開催される3つの展覧会を1つに束ね、それらを1つのシナリオに置いて物語るものとなっています。
　そのため、全体のシナリオを紹介する「プロローグ」を頭として、3つのプロジェクトとそれぞれの都市での展覧会のためのイントロ、現地の有識者による小論、日本の建築史家によるそれぞれのためのサマリー、さらにその後に共通する展示物とその解説を並べ、それらを全体のシナリオの「エピローグ」で挟む構成となっています。
　本書のこうした構成は、「プロローグ」にも書かれるように、本書の物理的なアウトプットである展覧会同士の関係を1冊の本のなかに取り込んだものです。

　This book combines three exhibitions held in different cities into one and puts them in one scenario.
　Therefore, with a "Prologue" that introduces the entire scenario in the first place, an introduction for three projects and exhibitions in each city, critiques by local experts, a summary for each exhibition by a Japanese architectural historian, after that, the common exhibits and their explanations are lined up. And they are placed between the "Prologue" and the "Epilogue" of the entire scenario.
　The structure of this book, as written in the "Prologue", incorporates the relationship between each exhibition, which is the physical output of this book, into one structure.

ひとつなぎの建築
Unity Architecture

3つの展覧会
3Exhibitions

Nation of Sorrow	Japanese Crossover-Architecture	Synesthesia Scenery
from Helsinki	from Berlin	from Weimar

イントロ、小論、サマリー
intro, critique, summary

イントロ、小論、サマリー
intro, critique, summary

イントロ、小論、サマリー
intro, critique, summary

18のオブジェクト
18Objects

a	b	c	r

共通のオブジェクト 及び その解説
Common objects and each explanation

3つのプロジェクト
3Projects

Xover-Architecture	Xover-Houses	Xover-Products

クロスオーバー・プロジェクト 及び その解説
Xover Projects and each explanation

Contents

Prologue

受容的能動性による
デザイン

Design by Receptive Activism

はじめに

　本書は、東京会場（在日本フィンランド
大使館）を最初の舞台としてフィンランド・
ヘルシンキ（アアルト大学）、ドイツ・ベ
ルリン（ベルリン工科大学）及びワイマー
ル（バウハウス大学ワイマール校）を会場
にこの１年余りをかけて開催される３つ
の展覧会自体を展示する展覧会を本の形に
まとめたものです。これらの試みは、フィ
ンランドと日本両国に共有可能なデザイン
様式を再発見し、両国の未来のデザインの
応答を促進させていくこと、さらに共有可

Introduction

　This book records the exhibitions which
start in Tokyo (Embassy of Finland in Japan).
It then travels to Helsinki, Finland (Aalto
University), Berlin, Germany (Technische
Universität Berlin), and Weimar, Germany
(Bauhaus-Universität, Weimar) in the coming
year. It is also an event that displays the
three exhibitions themselves. The exhibition
has two purposes. First, we will rediscover a
design style that both Finland and Japan
can share and promote a response to future
design in both countries. The other is to
universalize designs that Finland and Japan

能な「第三の場所」を発見し、その文脈から翻訳することでフィンランドと日本の両国で共有され得るデザインの普遍化を行うこと、の2点を目的としています。

そのため展覧会では、フィンランドと日本の2か国にドイツを加えた3か国・4会場にて日本の近現代建築の一部を抽出した同一の18のオブジェクトをそれぞれの場所性が持つ異なる文脈から紹介する方法を採ることにしました。加えて、東京ではそれぞれ互いに自立した異なる文脈を貫く道筋を見出し、その先に3つのプロジェクトを配置しました。

同一の展示物を展示する異なる3つの展覧会を展示する、という展覧会の構成を引いた本書の少々複雑な構成はこれらの理由に依っていることをご理解いただけますと幸いです。

受容的能動性によるデザイン

ここで注目したのは、フィンランド発祥のナショナル・ロマンティシズムの精神です。

従来のナショナル・ロマンティシズムは近代黎明期に勃興した印象様式の1つとされ、特に建築では地中海世界を中心としたヨーロッパの周縁部に伝播したアール・ヌーボー様式の地域主義的表現とされてきました。しかし、フィンランド各地での様々な調査や実地検分を行うにつれ、表層に現れた様式の奥に秘匿された本来の精神構造にこそ、フィンランド・日本両国の未来に賦活すべきデザインの普遍があることに思い至りました。このナショナル・ロマンティシズムを再発見する文脈は、ヘルシンキ会場の主題である「Nation of Sorrow」（哀

can share by discovering and interpreting designs from the context of a "third place".

For these reasons, we will introduce 18 identical objects representing parts of modern and contemporary Japanese architecture within different contexts according to locality of four venues in the three countries; Helsinki in Finland, Tokyo in Japan and Berlin, Weimar in Germany. Additionally, the Tokyo venue explores a path through different contexts, each independent of the other, to place the other three exhibitions ahead.

I hope you understand that these elements produce an exhibition and this book with a slightly complex structure, displaying three different exhibitions themselves with the same objects.

Design by Receptive Activism

The focus here is on the spirit of national romanticism that originated in Finland.

Conventional interpretations of national romanticism regard it as one of the impressionist styles that emerged in the early modern era, particularly in architecture. Some have interpreted national romanticism as a regionalist expression of the Mediterranean Art Nouveau style that spread to the periphery of Europe. However, while conducting surveys and field inspections in various parts of Finland, I realized that the universality of design that both Finland and Japan will activate in the future exists in the original mental structure hidden behind the superficial forms. The context of rediscovering national romanticism eventually led to the Helsinki venue's theme: Nation of Sorrow. As in the ancient Japanese meaning of the word, "sorrow" here also means "affection".

Throughout the 20th century, Finland

しきネーション）という価値観へと結実していきました。日本の古語での意味にもあるように、ここで言う「哀しみ」は、「愛しみ」でもあります。

20世紀を通じて東西陣営双方の軍事的、政治的、経済的な外圧に晒されるなかで、フィンランドはそれらをいなすことで乗り超えていく道を発見したのではないかと思います。そのためには、異なる考えを持った人々が互いに心を通わせ、他者の意見に耳を澄まし、その総意を表すものとしてデザインは必要不可欠なものでした。その結果、抑圧状態のなかであるデザインに到達するための過程がさらに次なるデザインを生み出す社会的基盤を形成する、そういう風土が育まれていったのだと思います。

こうしたフィンランドの社会が持つ根源的な性質を「受容的能動性」と捉え、独立期と近代黎明期が重なったフィンランドで生まれたナショナル・ロマンティシズムの基本的メカニズムであるとの結論に至りました。いわば日本の柔道の"巴投げ"のような、相手から掛けられた外圧を自身の背後へと受け流す力を利用して、実は投げているのは自分であるというデザインの有り様です。

独立以降の苦難の歴史のなかで、フィンランドは国を挙げてそのような態度を社会全体が持ち続けるというモデルを体現してきました。その極めて具体的で実務的な方法には、実は同じような境遇にある他の国や地域の「第三の場所」の人々にも当て嵌めて考えるのに十分普遍的なメカニズムがあります。

そのメカニズムを明らかにして言語化し多様な他者と共有することが、さらに2つ

confronted external military, political, and economic pressure from both the East and West and found a way to overcome these pressures. In short, design became essential for people with different ideas to communicate with each other, listen to the opinions of others, and express their consensus. As a result, I think that Finland developed a process of reaching a form of design in a state of oppression, which builds a social foundation for further generations of design.

I have concluded that Finnish society's fundamental nature is "receptive activism" and that it is the primary mechanism of the national romanticism born in Finland during the overlapping period of independence and the dawn of modernity. In other words, the mechanism is like the Tomoe-nage in Japanese judo, in which one wards off and reverses the power of an opponent's external pressure by throwing the challenger back.

In the country's painful history since its independence, Finnish society has embodied this attitude for design. The most concrete and practical way of doing so is through a universal mechanism to apply to people in "third places" in other countries and regions in similar circumstances.

Clarifying the mechanism, making it linguistic, and sharing it with diverse audiences spurs the other three exhibitions and Tokyo exhibition, which unites all three.

For this reason, I compare the generality and universality of Finnish design, which is a continuum of modern and contemporary design, with the modern and contemporary as the beginning of the modernism. Inevitably, the exhibits must be non-Finnish designs with expressions and techniques

の異なる場所での展覧会とそれら３つを束ねた展覧会を行うことの大義です。

　そのため、近代と現代が連続したフィンランドデザインが持つ総合性と普遍性を、モダニズムを始まりとする近現代に対峙させたいと考えました。必然的に、展示物は建築に専門化されていない表現や技術によるフィンランド以外のデザインであらねばなりません。フィンランド以外の場所にあるデザインのなかに同じメカニズムを見出せて初めてフィンランドのナショナル・ロマンティシズムは国際的に言語化されるからです。その結果として、今回の展覧会群では切り取られた日本の近現代建築のいくつかのシーンを例示しています。これらの日本のデザインの背景には、エリエル・サーリネン設計のヘルシンキ中央駅のドローイングと共に私が１年余りフィンランド各地を廻ってコレクションしたオブジェクト（立体造形物）とライト（光）のコラージュ・ドローイングを「Learning from Finlandia」として置くことにしました。

　「Nation of Sorrow」とは、このような受容的能動性によるデザインのメカニズムが適用可能なネーション（国、地域、集団など）を指す抽象名詞です。

　次に、そのメカニズムよって作られる建築を「クロスオーバー・アーキテクチュア」と呼んでいます。ベルリンでは、この文脈からヘルシンキ会場と同じ展示物を説明しています。クロスオーバーという枕詞は、「建築以外の分野のデザイン言語を用いた建築デザイン」を意味しています。その詳細は同会場に向けたイントロ文に譲ります

that are not specialized in architecture. Only when we find the same mechanism in designs outside Finland can we universalize and express Finnish national romanticism in design vocabulary. Thus, this exhibition illustrates several scenes of Japanese modern and contemporary architecture. In the background of these Japanese designs, I decided to place a drawing of Helsinki Central Railway Station designed by Eliel Saarinen and drawings of sculptures and lights that I had collected around Finland for over a year as Learning from Finlandia.

　"Nation of Sorrow" is an abstract noun referring to a nation (country, region, or group) to which one can apply such design mechanisms of receptive activism.

　Next, the architecture that this mechanism creates is called Crossover Architecture. The exhibition in Berlin will display the same exhibits as in the Helsinki venue. The word "crossover" denotes "architectural design using design vocabulary in a field other than architecture". The details appear in the introductory text at the Berlin venue. In Berlin, in particular, the exhibition aims to translate the mechanism by which Finnish national romanticism emerged in modern design theory without using its language or its unique social background.

　Finally, I call the spatial nature of this crossover architecture Synesthesia Scenery. In this meaning, spatial characteristics don't reside in space itself but within a mind that has sensed relationships between objects (ambiguous solids) that are not defined by functions. Synesthesia is a term in neurology that refers to a state in which a stimulus activates one of the five senses that, ordinarily, it would not have engaged. There

が、特にベルリンではフィンランドでナショナル・ロマンティシズムが生まれたメカニズムを、その言葉や特有の社会背景を用いずに近現代デザインの理論として言語化することを目的としています。

　最後に、そのクロスオーバー・アーキテクチュアの空間的性質を指して「共感覚空間」（シナスタジア・シーナリー）と呼んでいます。空間的性質は空間そのものではなく、機能によって定義されないオブジェクト（曖昧な立体）同士の間に働く作用関係を感知した人間の内側に生まれると考えたためです。共感覚とは、ある１つの刺激によって稼働する人間の五感のうち、それ以外の直接作用しないはずの別の五感が働いてしまう状態を指す神経学の用語です。このような人間の意識とオブジェクトの協働によって空間を再定義する場所として、世界初の近代建築学校であるバウハウス以上に歴史的な意義がある場所はないでしょう。

Unity Architecture への道

　このように、日本の東京でフィンランドのデザイン史観から見出された展示物＝オブジェクトがフィンランドを経由してドイツのベルリン、ワイマールへと異なる文脈を移り渡っていくに従い、３つの展覧会の主題もフィールド編：ネーション・オブ・ソロウ、理論編：クロスオーバー・アーキテクチュア、実践編：シナスタジア・シーナリュア、の３つのステップとして位置付けられることで、１本の深化した道筋を照らしています。

　共有可能な「第三の場所」を多数発見し、それらを「Nation of Sorrow」と総称し

is nowhere more historically significant than Bauhaus, the world's first modern school of architecture, to redefine space through this collaboration of human consciousness and objects.

A Path to Unity Architecture

In this way, the Tokyo venue explores objects as exhibits from the historical viewpoint of Finnish design. As the objects move through different contexts to Berlin and Weimar in Germany via Finland, they illuminate a single deepened path. The themes of the three exhibitions can be positioned as three steps: Nation of Sorrow as a field edition, Crossover Architecture as a theory edition, and Synesthesia Scenery as a practice edition.

I have found many "third places" to share, and I called them Nation of Sorrow. If we recall that Finland, Germany, and Japan were defeated in World War II, it may be inevitable that we find a common motivation for design through receptive activism among these countries.

It would be great if the ideas presented in this book were to grow into a platform for millions of people to interact with design in the future.

In my recent work, I started a design project called Xover (crossover) architecture, houses, and products. Please visit the Watanabe Laboratory website to learn more. http://www.f.waseda.jp/watanabetaishi/xover_theory.html

Beyond these practices, we are trying to approach an architectural ideal called "Unity Architecture" (a string of architecture).

"A string of architecture" refers to the overall outline of myriad causalities that work between different things in different

たいと述べましたが、フィンランド・ドイツ・日本の共通点がいずれも先の大戦の敗戦国であることにも思いを馳せるならば、これらの国々に共通して受容的能動性によるデザインのモチベーションが見出されることも必然的なことなのかもしれません。

ここでお見せするアイディアが、未来の無数の人々のデザインを通じた応答のプラットフォームに育っていくならば、これほどの悦びはありません。

最近の私自身の取り組みとしては、Xover（クロスオーバー）-Architecture、-Houses、-Products といったデザインプロジェクトを立ち上げ、少しずつですが実践し始めています。本書や展覧会に加えて渡邊研究室のウェブサイトもご覧いただければ幸いです。（http://www.f.waseda.jp/watanabetaishi/xover_theory.html）

こうした実践の先に、ユニティ・アーキテクチュア（ひとつなぎの建築）という建築の理想に迫る努力を続けています。

「ひとつなぎの建築」とは、地球上の異なる場所の異なる事柄の間に働いている無数の因果律の全体の輪郭を指しています。それは、時に社会的に共有された心象の連鎖が空間化されたソーシャルマインド・スケープとして立ち現れます。

19 世紀末から 20 世紀初頭にかけて、建築の近代は専ら世界の模型であることによって、その近代建築としての全体性を獲得しようとしました。それに対して「ひとつなぎの建築」は、日常生活のなかにもある世界との因果関係を捉え、限られた空間の記述からその因果律の全体の輪郭を描こうとするものです。ですから、劇場を始め

locations. Sometimes a string of socially-shared ideas emerges as a spatialized social mindscape.

From the end of the 19th century to the beginning of the 20th century, modern architecture sought to acquire its totality by being a model of the universe. On the other hand, the concept of "a string of architecture" captures causal relationships with the universe in everyday life and attempts to draw the entire outline of causality from the description in a limited space. Therefore, this concept is completely the opposite of modern architecture as a universal model, such as a theater. The exhibition's method of presenting the same exhibits in different locational contexts and bundling them together in parallel with the other locations aims to express "a string of architecture".

In other words, the intent here is to treat each of the three independent exhibitions as its mirror image through "a string of exhibitions" and to exhibit the very structure of the whole exhibition. The exhibits aim to re-import and reinterpret fragments of modern and contemporary Japanese architecture, interpreted according to local contexts in foreign countries, within the Japanese context. The exhibition also intends to be relativistic by viewing the exhibition's context from the Finnish Embassy in Japan, located in "Finland in Tokyo", which accepts national romanticism without friction. In short, the exhibition itself has a double structure.

In view of this duality, the introductory message for each venue has a consistent structure even in different contexts.

1. Problems

とした世界模型としての近代建築とは正反対なものと言えます。同一の展示物を異なる場所性の文脈によって紹介し、それらを束ねてそのいずれとも異なる場所で並列して見せるという展覧会の方法はその初歩的な試みです。

すなわち、それぞれが独立した３つの展覧会を「ひとつなぎの展覧会」によって自らの鏡像として相対化し、その構造自体を展示することがここでは意図されています。展示物については日本の近現代建築の断片が外国での現地の文脈によって読み直されたものを逆輸入して再び日本的なるものの文脈に読み直す、また、場所性についても東京にありながらナショナル・ロマンティシズムが摩擦なく着地できるフィンランド大使館という「日本のなかのフィンランド」から展覧会の文脈そのものを並列して眺めることで相対化する、という二重の構図があるわけです。

こうした二重の構図を見据えて、各会場ごとのイントロ文はそれぞれ異なる文脈のなかにおいても一貫して

1. 問題の所在
2. 具体的な方法
3. 展示内容説明
4. 日本という
   バックグラウンドの特殊性
5. 展望

という共通した構成で書かれています。

東京を除く全ての展覧会は 2020 年の春夏に開催される予定だったものが、新型コ

2. Concrete measures for the problems
3. Description of the contents
4. Peculiarity of the background of Japan
5. Conclusions

Except for Tokyo, all of the exhibitions were scheduled for the spring and summer of 2020, but the COVID-19 pandemic forced a significant delay of over a year. Although I was very disappointed by their repeated postponements, our daily lives throughout the pandemic showed that the virus had a mechanism that led all people to new social mindscapes.

We should have acquired this environment in a more positive way. As for myself, when the pandemic has ended, I will move to Finland, Germany, Japan, and other "third places", such as Asia and the Middle East, to aim for unity architecture by focusing on familiar objects in front of me as much as possible in each place. I believe that doing so achieves the ultimate state of synthesis in "Design by Receptive Activism".

I hope that you will experience even a part of it through this book and exhibitions.

Finally, I would like to express my sincere gratitude to all those who agreed to the exhibition's purpose and allowed me to display their exhibits, and all the co-workers in Japan, Finland, and Germany who helped realize the exhibition and write and produce the books and catalogs.

May 2021
Taishi WATANABE

ロナウイルス感染症の世界的流行によって1年以上の大幅な延期を余儀なくされたものです。度重なる開催の延期は私自身大変残念なものでしたが、コロナ禍の生活は世界中の全ての人々にその人が所属する社会なりの新しいソーシャルマインド・スケープをもたらすメカニズムをウィルスが持っていたことを示したとも言えます。

　本来ならば人類はこの環境をもっとポジティブな方法によって獲得すべきであったでしょう。私自身、コロナ禍が収束した後には、自らの身体をフィンランド、ドイツ、日本、さらにアジアや中東などのその他の「第三の場所」へと移動させながら、その場所々々でできうる限り目の前の身近な対象に執着することで、ユニティ・アーキテクチュアを目指して行きたいと思っています。それこそが「受容的能動性によるデザイン」が持つ総合性の究極の有り様ではないか、と信じているからです。

　本書とこれらの展覧会を通じて、その片鱗でもみなさんに触れていただけることを願ってやみません。

　最後に、このような趣旨に賛同してくださり、展示物を出品してくださった方々、展覧会の実現と書籍やカタログの執筆・作成にご協力いただいた日本、フィンランド、ドイツの全ての協働者に厚く御礼申し上げます。

2021 年 5 月
渡邊大志

3 ———— Xover Projects

Projects

クロスオーバー・プロジェクト

　Xover とは、1. 国境・国籍、2. 空間モデュール、3. 機能、4. 技術（分野・職人）の 4 つの要素を横断するデザインです。これは、Learning from Finlandia の成果を私たちなりに展開したものです。さらに、渡邊研究室では Xover-Architecture、-Houses、-Products といった 3 つのデザインプロジェクトを起こすことで、都市、建築、住宅、家具といったスケールを横断して Xover という考え方を拡張し、実践していきます。日本・フィンランド・ドイツをメインマーケットとし、受容的能動性による共通のメカニズムを持つネーションに、一連の展覧会で考えたアイディアに基づいたデザインを発信していく試みです。

　Xover is the design crossovering composed by the following four elements, 1. National borders and nationalities, 2. Space modules, 3. Functions, 4. Technologies (Fields & Craftsmen). This is our own development of the results of Learning from Finlandia. In addition, Watanabe Laboratory will expand and practice the idea of Xover across scales such as city, architecture, housing, and furniture by starting three design projects such as Xover-Architecture, -Houses, and -Products. With Japan-Finland-Germany as the main market, This is an attempt to send a design based on the ideas considered in this exhibition series to Nation, which has a common mechanism of receptive activity.

Xover-Architecture

「Helsinki south harbour project」、渡邊大志研究室 コラージュ。
"Helsinki south harbour project"collage by Taishi WATANABE Lab.

Xover-Houses

「13℃ houses」、渡邊大志研究室 コラージュ。 "13℃ houses"collage by Taishi WATANABE Lab.

Xover-Products

「Homo sapiens and objects」、渡邊大志研究室 コラージュ。
"Homo sapiens and objects" collage by Taishi WATANABE Lab.

Xover 3つのプロジェクト
3 Xover Projects

Xover-Architecture

　ヘルシンキ港・南港の将来計画及び一部建築デザインの提案です。本プロジェクトは、ユルヨ・ソタマーと渡邊大志を含む日本・フィンランド協同チームによって進行しています。

　現在のヘルシンキ中央駅周辺を中心とする文化的ゾーンは、ビックデータを活用したスマートシティのモデル作りが実践されています。私たちは、これと併存する形で、ヘルシンキ市のもう1つの歴史的中心部であるヘルシンキ港・南港を約100年のフィンランドデザインの蓄積と豊富な木材資源・技術を活用した「Health-Eco City」のモデルとしていくことを提案しています。

Xover-Architecture

　This is a project for the future plan of port of Helsinki south harbour and some architectural designs. This project is carried out by a Japan-Finland cooperative team, including Yrjö Sotamaa and Taishi Watanabe.

　In the current cultural zone centered around Helsinki central station, smart city models using big data are being practiced. As a parallel model of this, we are proposing to use port of Helsinki south harbour, another historical center of Helsinki, as a model of "Health-Eco City" that utilizes the accumulation of Finnish design for about 100 years and abundant wood resources and technology.

木によって作られる健康環境都市の諸機能
Actions for Health-Eco city made by wood

1. 建築とデザイン / Architecture & Design
2. 健康食品、魚市場 / Health Food ,Fish Market
3. 紫外線療法 / UV Lighting Therapy
4. サウナ / Sauna
5. コーヒー博物館 / Coffee Museum
6. 多様な人々のための健康保険 /
   Health Care Insurance for Diverse People
7. 緑化 / Greening
8. スチームサウナシップ / Steam Sauna Ship
9. バイオマス発電、バードハウス /
   Biomass Power Generation, Bird House
10. セーリング / Sailing
11. フィットネス / Fitness

フィンランドの白樺と松の木を様々な形態（インフラ、船、建築、道具、バイオ燃料など）に加工・活用することで生まれる複数の産業が連なった「ウッドベルト」を新たな健康エコロジー産業のショーケースとします。

この健康エコロジー産業を通してデザインマーケットの主導権を取り戻し、バルト海文化圏のなかでフィンランドが先導的地位を再び担っていく未来を目指します。これは、ヘルシンキ港において国家のアイデンティティーを表現する新しいソーシャルランドスケープです。

Xover-Houses

私たちはフィンランドと日本の住宅生産システムに共通の寸法体系を見出しました。日本では 4 × 8 判と呼ばれ、フィンランドではスタンダードサイズとされる、1200 × 2400 mm のモジュールです。Xover-Houses は、これを共通のモジュールとしてフィンランドと日本の双方に建設可能な住宅を供給する試みです。

具体的なデザイン対象は室内外の温度としました。0℃ (屋外) と 24℃ (屋内) の中間に 13℃の領域をデザインすることによって、内外の中間領域で行われる生活の豊かさを獲得することを意図しています。日本をはじめとして、従来の都市住宅は、その住環境の平均的な快適さを求め、室内温度の平準化を図ってきました。1 年のなかで -20℃から +25℃までの外気温の変化があるフィンランドでも又、ディストリクトヒーティング（地域熱供給）によって室内温度が常に 24℃に保たれています。しかしながら、その一方でフィンランドの人

The "Wood Belt", which is a series of multiple industries created by processing and utilizing Finnish birch and pine trees in various forms (infrastructure, ships, architecture, tools, biofuels, etc.), will be a showcase for the new health ecology industry.

Through this health ecology industry, we aim that Finland regains control of the design market and takes a leading position in the Baltic Sea culture. This will be a new social landscape that expresses the national identity in port of Helsinki.

Xover-Houses

We have found a common module for Finnish and Japanese housing production systems. It is a size of 1200 x 2400 mm, which is called the 4 x 8 size in Japan and the standard size in Finland. The project of Xover-Houses is an attempt to provide residences that can be built in both Finland and Japan with this size as the module.

The specific design target is the temperature of indoor and outdoor. By designing an area of 13 °C between 0 °C (outdoor) and 24 °C (indoor), it is intended to acquire a wealth of life applied in the intermediate area. Today's urban housing, including Japan, is trying to level the indoor temperature in search of the average comfort of its living environment. Also in Finland, where changes in the outside temperature range from -20 to +25 through a year, the inside temperature is kept 24°C by the district heating. However, on the other hand, Finnish people try to go out even in a harsh winter, and like to live with nature. This attitude of trying to coexist with nature and the surrounding environment is very important. The project of Xover-Houses pays attention to this point, and we aim to share

たちは、厳しい寒さのなかでもできる限り外に出て、自然とともに暮らすことを好みます。この自然や周囲の環境と共生しようと心掛ける態度はとても重要です。Xover-Houses はこの点に注目し、日本ーフィンランド両国の異なる気候のなかに共通して見出される 13℃の中間領域を持つ住宅とその生産システムの共有を目的としています。

Xover-Products

Xover-Products は、今や固有の少数生産システムでしか生まれることが困難なデザインの社会性を念頭に置きながら、国際チーム（建築家・デザイナー・職人・工場）と共に、ものが機能をもつ直前の「曖昧な立体」を製作・販売するプロジェクトです。

Xover-Products は、1. 使う人によって色々な使い方ができる、2. 同じデザインで他の素材が選べる、3. 慣れた技術から新しいデザインを発見する、という３つの考えに基づいています。そのシンボルである「χ」は、現存する日本最古の木造建築である法隆寺五重塔に用いられた鍛造釘（Xover-Product No.000）に由来します。この鍛造釘は、当時の刀剣や祭具などを作っていた職人がその技術を転用して製作した日本でほぼ初めての建築専用部品です。法隆寺五重塔は、この鍛造釘が隠し釘として使われることで 1000 年以上もの間建ち続けています。こうした従来の分野を横断する技術やデザインを想起させる曖昧な立体を制作することを目指しています。実際の商品や詳細は、Xover-Products 販売サイトをご覧ください。(http://www.f.waseda.jp/watanabetaishi/xover.html)

houses that have 13 intermediate areas and their production system, which are commonly found in the different climates of both Japan and Finland.

Xover-Products

Xover-Products is a project to produce and sell an "ambiguous solid" just before something has a function, together with an international team (architects, designers, craftsmen, factories), keeping in mind the sociality of design only born from a unique minority production system now.

The project of Xover-Products is based on the following three ideas, 1. The object can be used in various ways depending on the users, 2. Users can choose other materials with the same design of one object, 3. We can discover new designs from familiar technologies. The symbol of "χ" came from the forged nails (Xover-Product No.000) used in the five-storied pagoda in Horyuji temple that is the oldest existing wooden architecture in Japan. These forged nails are almost the first architectural product in Japan, and it was made by repurposing the technology of blacksmiths who were making swords and rituals objects. The five-storied pagoda in Horyuji temple has been standing for more than 1000 years because these forging nails are placed in invisible places as hidden nails. We try to produce "ambiguous solids" that make us imagine such technologies or designs crossing over the conventional fields. You can see the actual products and the details on the Xover-Products sales website. (http://www.f.waseda.jp/watanabetaishi/xover.html)

3

Exhibitions

1

Nation of Sorrow

ユニティ・アーキテクチュア／フィールド編
ヘルシンキ展

Unity Architecture / Field Edition
Exhibition in Helsinki

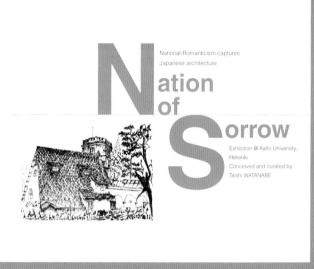

National-Romanticism captures
Japanese architecture

N
ation
of
S
orrow

Exhibition @ Aalto University,
Helsinki
Conceived and curated by
Taishi WATANABE

ヘルシンキ展カタログ表紙
Catalog Cover for the Exhibition in Helsinki

　ヘルシンキでの「Nation of Sorrow」展の扉絵に
は、私が現地でスケッチしたアクセリ・ガッレン＝
カッレラ自邸（現在は同氏ミュージアム）の画を採
用しています。
　ガッレン＝カッレラはフィンランドのナショナ
ル・ロマンティシズムの理念とそのデザイン様式を
実質的に創造した張本人と目されます。自らがデザ
インした自邸は内外にいくつもの様式が折衷してお
り、その結果として様々なデザイン分野の技術が横
断して形作られています。その姿と技術の関係性の
あり様は「Nation of Sorrow」におけるデザインの
原風景です。

For the frontispiece of the "Nation of Sorrow" exhibition
in Helsinki, I used the sketch of Akseli Gallen-Kallela's
house (currently his museum) that I sketched when I was
staying in Helsinki.
　Gallen-Kallela is considered to be the person who
practically created the idea of Finnish National
Romanticism and its design style. His own home,
designed by himself, is a mix of styles both inside and
outside, resulting in the cross-cutting of techniques from a
variety of design disciplines. The relationship between
this appearance and technology is the original landscape
of the design in "Nation of Sorrow".

Introduction

「Nation of Sorrow」 という戦略

Strategy of the "Nation of Sorrow"

渡邊大志
Taishi WATANABE

　ヘルシンキでの展覧会は、フィンランド
で生まれたナショナル・ロマンティシズム
のメカニズムを構造的に理解し、その視点
から見た日本の近現代建築のいくつかを紹
介するものです。

　その目的は、現代に生きる私たちを取り
巻くデザイン環境についてその源泉に今一
度立ち返り、社会の未来へとつながるデザ
インの思想的プラットフォームを再構築す
ることにあります。

　ご存知の通り、フィンランドは 1917 年

The exhibition in Helsinki introduces
some of Japan's modern and contemporary
architecture from the viewpoint of a
structural understanding of the mechanism
of Finland's national romanticism.

This project revisits the design
environment's origins that surrounds us
today to reconstruct an ideological platform
of design that paves the way for the future of
society.

Finland became independent in 1917
and is one of the world's younger countries.
Furthermore, Finland increased its

に独立を果たした世界でも若い国の1つです。しかし、フィンランドの社会は1950-70年代におけるデザイン産業の創出によって世界的に勃興し、今日まで続くデザイン市場そのものを形成する大きな原動力となりました。結果として、戦後のフィンランドの社会全体がデザインを輸出する方策の観点から形作られたといっても過言ではありません。

その一方で、近年ではその他の後進のデザイン産業国がその覇権をうかがい、多くの類似商品が世界各地でより安価に生産されるなど、往時の隆盛を経たフィンランドのデザイン産業は次なる戦略を必要とする画期を迎えています。

これまでナショナル・ロマンティシズムはそのデザイン産業の黎明期に当たる1910-20年代に芽生えたフィンランド特有の時代精神として理解されてきました。フィンランドのナショナル・アイデンティティを形作る一方で、同時代の西欧の国々とは一線を画したその表現様式は、ナショナル・ロマンティシズムを北欧にある1地方特有のものと解釈させたのです。

確かにその表現様式自体にも未だに見るべきものがありますが、ここで問題としたいのは度重なる戦争による時代背景も含めてどのようなメカニズムがナショナル・ロマンティシズムという思想体系を生み出したのかという点です。それが明らかになれば、ナショナル・ロマンティシズムは世界のその他の国や地域、異なる宗教の人々にも普遍的に共有可能なデザイン（表現文化）の思想となり得ると考えました。そしてそれはナショナル・ロマンティシズムとは違った名前で呼ばれるべき、新しい概念です。

international presence from 1950s through 70s by creating the design industry; as such, the country has been a significant driving force for creating the global design market. In fact, the whole society of post-war Finland was shaped by the viewpoint of exporting designs.

Today, Finland's design industry, which was once prosperous, has reached a period in which a powerful strategy is needed because other less-developed countries' design industries want to take on its hegemony. Additionally, many similar products to Finland's are produced more cheaply in other parts of the world.

Until now, national romanticism has been understood as the Finnish zeitgeist that emerged in the 1910s and 1920s at the dawn of the design industry. While shaping Finland's national identity, its style of expression (which was distinct from Western countries at the time), led to the interpretation of national romanticism as peculiar to one region of Northern Europe.

While it is true that the style of expression itself is still worth seeing, I would like to ask at this exhibition what kind of mechanism (including the historical background of repeated wars), created national romanticism. If this were made clear, then national romanticism could become an idea in design (expressive culture) that could be universally shared by people from different religions and countries. Furthermore, it could be a new concept and should be called by a name distinct from national romanticism.

From this perspective, it is interesting to review how Finland's national romanticism was not created gradually by an unconscious will of the masses but was created deliberately by a few identifiable

この点から改めてフィンランドにおけるナショナル・ロマンティシズムを見直してみると、それが無意識の集団意思によって次第に現れたものではなく、数名の特定された表現者たちによって意図的に作り出された概念であったことはとても興味深いことです。

画家のアクセリ・ガッレン=カッレラ、音楽家のジャン・シベリウス、指揮者のロバート・カヤヌスの３人が「シンポジオン」と呼ぶ夜の飲み会から生まれたアイデアであったことを、ガッレン=カッレラ自身が描いた同名の絵画は私たちに想像させます。

そこに建築家は描かれていません。

ナショナル・ロマンティシズムを語る上で欠かすことができないエリエル・サーリネンが建築の分野でそれを実践していったことにも、彼のクライアントであったガッレン=カッレラの影響が指摘されています。しかし、ある「シンポジオン」の夜、建築家が同席していなかったという偶然（あるいは必然）が、むしろ今となっては建築の専門化によって閉塞しつつある建築の未来を大きく拓いていく可能性を示しています。

その現代的意義とは、フィンランドの特殊性を用いることなく「建築のデザイン言語によらないデザインによって作られた建築」の手法とそのデザイン思想を新しく構築していくということです。

このことを踏まえ、本展覧会ではナショナル・ロマンティシズムの表現様式を以下の３つの特質によって再定義することにしました。

expressionists.

A painting of the same name as its artist, Akseli Gallen-Kallela, lets us imagine that the concept of national romanticism was born at an evening party called "Symposion" attended by the artist Gallen-Kallela, the musician Jean Sibelius, and the conductor Robert Kajanus. But no architect was included in the painting.

Eliel Saarinen's architecture, which was an essential element of establishing national romanticism, was influenced by his client, Gallen-Kallela. However, the "coincidence", or "necessity", that an architect was not present at the "Symposion" shows the possibility of opening the future of architecture up, which is currently blocked by the specialization of architecture.

The modern significance of national romanticism is that it does not use the peculiarities of Finland's design to develop new methods, and the design concepts of "architecture made by design not in the language of architecture".

As a result, we have decided to redefine the style expression of national romanticism in this exhibition with the following three characteristics:

1. The design replaces the attitude of accepting external pressure with one's own expression.
2. The design does not have a single mode of expression or a particular field of expression.
3. An idea that accepts oneself as a global minority.

It is important to note that the nationalism of self-display, which excludes others, is actually the same mechanism as the

1. 外圧を受容する態度そのものを自らの表現に置き換えるためのデザイン
2. そのデザインは初めから唯一の表現様式や特定の表現分野を持たない
3. 自分自身が世界的にマイノリティであることを受け入れる思想

　ここで留意したいことは、他者を排除する自己顕示というナショナリズムはその抗うべき外圧と実は同じメカニズムであるという点です。そのためナショナリズムはより強いナショナリズムに負かされる構図から逃れ得ず、結果として生き残ったナショナリズムがグローバリズムを形成する以外にありません。上記の定義では、ナショナル・ロマンティシズムはナショナリズムと異なるメカニズムであることを明確にしておきたいと思います。

　その上で本展では、日本最古の現存する木造建築物である法隆寺五重塔（6世紀）に用いられた鍛造釘を復元し、これを日本の建築文化をナショナル・ロマンティシズムのメカニズムから捉える具体的なマイルストーンとしました。この塔は現代でいうところの超高層ビルであり、特に地震が多い日本で古代にこれだけ高い木造の塔を建設するためには高度な技術が必要でした。1400年ほどの時を経てもなお、現在日本で一番高い塔である東京スカイツリーにその構造原理が採用されたほどです。その五重塔を支える木組みの数々には、外から見えない方法で鍛造釘が仕込まれていることが現在分かっています。
　その鍛造釘が作られた現場を想像してみてください。このような建築を作った経験

external pressure to be resisted. Therefore, nationalism should be exposed to a mechanism that is defeated by a stronger nationalism; rather, nationalism that will survive must conform to globalism. This definition clarifies that national romanticism is a different mechanism than nationalism.

　In this exhibition, we restored forged nails used in the five-story pagoda of the Horyuji Temple built in the sixth century (which is Japan's oldest existing wooden building) and made the forged nail a concrete milestone in understanding Japanese architectural culture from the mechanism of national romanticism. The pagoda is a modern skyscraper, and in ancient times it required advanced technology, especially in earthquake-prone Japan. Even after fourteen hundred years, the tower's structural principle has been adopted in Tokyo Skytree, which is Japan's tallest tower. The wooden frames supporting the five-story pagoda contain forged nails that cannot be seen from the outside.
　Imagine the workplace where the forged nails were made. Not only were there no craftsmen with experience constructing such buildings, but also there must have been many craftsmen who usually made swords and ritual equipment. This suggests that building truly unknown architecture requires skills and craftsmen that do not specialize in known architecture. Meanwhile, as can be seen from the fact that each restored forged nail has a unique shape, the standardization of manufacturing methods is not necessarily a useful method for mass-producing identical products (you can still see it in products such as Iittala, in that it rarely appears in industrial design). These differences are not of quality, but of the

を持つ職人が誰もいないばかりか、普段は刀や祭具などを作っていた職人が多くいたに違いありません。このことは、本当に未知の建築を作るということは、既知の建築に専門化していない技術と職人が必要であるという真理を物語っています。それと同時に、復元された1本1本の鍛造釘がそれぞれ異なる独特な形状を持つことからも分かるように、製法の標準化が必ずしも全く同一の製品を大量生産する方法ではないという原理を示してもいます（それはIittalaの製品などに今も見ることができますが、日本の工業デザインに現れることはほぼありません）。それらの違いは質の違いではなく、工業化のなかにもあり得る個性なのです。

　そのようにして建築の分野以外の理屈（技術と職人）でできた建築は、当然そのデザインも未知なものとして現れます。このように法隆寺五重塔の鍛造釘を「他分野による工業化のなかで現れた個性」として捉え、本展では一貫してこれと同様の性質を見ることができる日本の近現代建築の異なる方法と姿のいくつかを取り上げています。

　私の母国である日本は、フィンランドと同様に先の大戦を枢軸国側の敗戦国として迎えました。フィンランドの終戦がソ連への敗戦であったのと同様に、日本の終戦はアメリカへの敗戦でした。そのため、戦後の東京はニューヨークに代表される巨大な商業消費都市として復興されました。沖縄を除いて物理的な占領をまぬがれた反面で、戦後の日本の風景は政治的・経済的に戦勝国側の論理で復興されました。それで

individuality that can occur in industrialization.

　Architecture that was constructed using a logic other than architecture (i.e., skill and craftsmanship) naturally shows its design that has not been seen before. Thus, the forged nails of the five-story pagoda of the Horyuji Temple are regarded as "Individuality that emerged in industrialization in other fields"; this exhibition introduces some different methods and forms of modern and contemporary Japanese architecture in which similar properties to the forged nails can be seen consistently.

　My home country, Japan, was defeated in World War II, being on the side of the Axis powers, like Finland. Just as Finland lost to the Soviet Union, Japan lost to the United States. As such, after World War II, Tokyo was reconstructed as a huge commercial consumption city like New York. Japan was able to avoid a military occupation, except the Okinawa region; however, post-war Japan was reconstructed politically and economically by the logic of victorious countries. Despite the reconstruction, Japan has an old history with a traditional culture. Its national system centered on the emperor for more than on thousand years, and Japan's traditional performing arts give non-Japanese this awareness. Additionally, many Japanese people regard Japan as a historical and traditional country. However, because many traditional performing arts have their roots in China and Korea, traditional Japanese design may not necessarily be seen as encompassing Japan's national identity.

　Despite this, the thoughts and expressions of national romanticism did not actually emerge in post-war Japan, much

も、世界では日本は伝統文化を持った歴史ある国とよく言われます。1000年以上続く天皇制の存在や伝統芸能などは外国の人にそうしたイメージを抱かせるでしょうし、日本人にも自分たちの国を歴史ある伝統的な国と思っている人は少なくないと思います。しかし、伝統芸能の多くが中国や朝鮮半島からの伝播にルーツがあるように、日本古来のデザインにナショナル・アイデンティティを視れるとは限りません。

それにも関わらず、実際には戦後の日本ではナショナル・ロマンティシズムの思想と表現が芽吹くことはなく、ましてや多くの人々を巻き込んだ集団意思として形成されることはありませんでした。その理由は、身の回りの風景が外から来た価値観に覆われても、なお自国や民族のアイデンティティはその歴史と伝統によって担保されていると信じていたからに他なりません。その歴史的状況から、日本には文化的ナショナリズムは勃興し得たとしてもナショナル・ロマンティシズムを育む自覚は生まれにくかったと言えます。

しかしながら、今日ではグローバリズムと呼ばれるに至った戦勝国側のより強いナショナリズムによって戦後の風景が再構築されていくなかで、世界的なマイノリティであった当時の日本の人々にもフィンランドの人たちの「Sisu」と似たような精神がどこかにあったに違いありません。本展で紹介する日本の近現代デザインのほとんどは、まさにその渦中にあった時代の日本の風景に立ち上げられたものです。そこには、西ヨーロッパを引き合いに出すことなくそのデザインアイデンティティをどう説明し、生み出すかという試行錯誤の表れを見

less were they formed by a collective will involving many people. This is because even though the things and ideas around us in Japan are completely influenced by foreign values, we still believe that our national and ethnic identities are secured by history and traditions. In light of this historical circumstance, it can be assumed that even if cultural nationalism could have risen to prominence in Japan, it was difficult for Japan to foster national romanticism.

However, because the post-war landscape was rebuilt by the stronger nationalism of victorious countries (which is now called globalism), there is no doubt that Japanese people, who were minorities around the world at the time, might have a similar spirit to the "Sisu" of Finnish people. Most modern and contemporary Japanese designs introduced in this exhibition were created based on Japan's landscape at that time. They also show the process of trial and error in how they explained and created its design identity without reference to Western Europe. However, it has also been pointed out that the stream of Japanese designs was so small and hidden that it was difficult to recognize unless it was intentionally cut out and presented again as designs independent of the mainstream.

In this way, it seems that Japan, like Finland, is a potential place where the mechanism of national romanticism could be born. Furthermore, we may find many other places in the world where similar mechanisms could work. I would like to label such countries, regions, and groups as "Nation of Sorrow".

In this case, the word "Sorrow" does not refer to the physical destruction caused by war or disaster; rather, it is a positive form of

ることもできます。ただし、それらは本来の全体像から独立したデザインとして意図的に切り出して再提示しなければ見えにくいほど、か細い伏流であったということもまた指摘されるのです。

このように考えを馳せてみると、日本もまたフィンランドと同様に本来はそのナショナル・ロマンティシズムのメカニズムが生まれ得た場所であると思えてきます。さらには、世界には他にも同様のメカニズムが働き得る場所を多く発見できるかもしれません。そのような国、地域、集団を指して「Nation of Sorrow」と呼んでみたいと思います。

ここでの「Sorrow」という言葉は、戦争や災害などによる物理的な破壊を指すのではありません。「Sisu」のような、その痛みを受け入れながらもそれを次なる未来への方策へと読み替えていけるだけの深淵さを持った、そして楽観や忘却による開き直りとも異なる前向きな「哀しみ」を言っています。本当の「哀しみ」がない場所に人間は暮らすことができず、そのため「哀しみ」は常にクリエーションの源泉なのです。

このような「Nation of Sorrow」の考えは、フィンランドという場所に今も潜在するナショナル・ロマンティシズムのメカニズムを世界でマイノリティと考えられる場所や状況に重ね見ることで、そこから生まれ得るデザインの世界を新たに構築するための戦略です。ですので、そこに生きる人々の存在は欠かせません。フィンランドのみなさんだけでなくどの国や地域出身の

"sorrow", such as "Sisu". "Sisu" is deep enough to accept pain but translates the pain into actions for the future and is different from the kind of recovery that comes from optimism and forgetting. People cannot live in places where there is no real sorrow; furthermore, sorrow is always a creative source.

This concept of a "Nation of Sorrow" is a strategy for creating a new perspective about design that can emerge from superimposing the mechanism of national romanticism that still underlies Finland onto places and situations considered to be minority in the world. Therefore, the existence of people living there is essential for "Nation of Sorrow". I hope that not only people in Finland, but also people from all countries and regions, will observe the different architectural methods and expressions produced in other countries (such as Japan) and compare them to the environment in which they were born and raised.

I also aspire for this exhibition to be an opportunity for people to reexamine the structure of national romanticism, which is the cultural basis of Finnish society, and examine a universal design strategy for the future.

みなさんにも、それぞれが生まれ育ってき
た環境になぞらえながら日本という他国で
出力された異なる手法と表現を観察してい
ただきたく思います。

　その結果として、本展覧会がフィンラン
ドの文化的基盤であるナショナル・ロマン
ティシズムを改めて構造的に見定め、そこ
から普遍的な未来のデザイン戦略を鑑みて
いく契機となれば大変嬉しく思います。

アクセリ・ガッレン＝カッレラ（1865-1931）『シンポジオン』
1894年、油絵、ゴスタ・セウラキウス美術財団蔵。画面左から、
アクセリ・ガッレン＝カッレラ、オスカー・メリカント、ロバー
ト・カヤヌス、ジャン・シベリウス。

Gallen-Kallela, Akseli (1865-1931), *Symposion*, 1894, Oil on canvas ©
Gösta Serlachius Fine Arts Foundation. From left, Akseli Gallen-Kallela,
Oskar Merikanto, Robert Kajanus and Jean Sibelius.

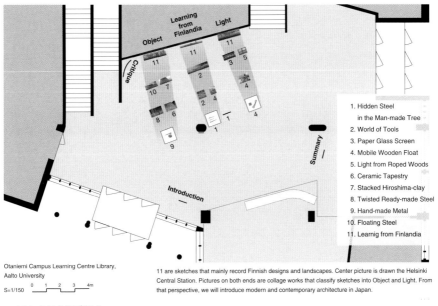

Learning from Finlandia

Object

Light

Critique

11
11
11

3
5

1
2
4

10
7
5
4

8
6
2
4

9
1
1

Introduction

Summary

1. Hidden Steel
   in the Man-made Tree
2. World of Tools
3. Paper Glass Screen
4. Mobile Wooden Float
5. Light from Roped Woods
6. Ceramic Tapestry
7. Stacked Hiroshima-clay
8. Twisted Ready-made Steel
9. Hand-made Metal
10. Floating Steel
11. Learnig from Finlandia

Otaniemi Campus Learning Centre Library,
Aalto University

S=1/150   0 1 2 3 4m

11 are sketches that mainly record Finnish designs and landscapes. Center picture is drawn the Helsinki Central Station. Pictures on both ends are collage works that classify sketches into Object and Light. From that perspective, we will introduce modern and contemporary architecture in Japan.

ヘルシンキ展会場デザイン Exhibition-gallery Diagram
アアルト大学オタニエミキャンパス／ラーニングセンター・ライブラリー Otaniemi Campus Learning Centre Library, AALTO University

Critique

見えないものを見る

Try to see what you cannot see

ユルヨ・ソタマー

アアルト大学名誉教授
フィンランドセンター名誉会長
日本フィンランドデザイン協会創設者

Yrjö SOTAMAA

Professor Emeritus, Aalto University
Honorary Chairman, The Finnish Institute in Japan
Founder, The Japan Finland Design Association JFDA

息子のキヴィは、アート・デザイン・建築において重要な「摩擦」という思想について多くのことを話してくれました。摩擦なしに円滑に働き動作する解決策を、デザイナーである私たちは度々目指すことがあります。これは、アート・デザイン・建築を考察するときの実用的または機能主義的な観点です。もちろん、それによれば世界は大きな問題や障害なしに機能するはずです。

アート・デザイン・建築は人類の発達に

My son Kivi has been talking to me much about friction as an important idea in art, design and architecture. As designers we often aim at solutions which run and work smoothly, without any friction. This a pragmatic or functionalist way of looking at art, design and architecture. The world should function, of course, without big problems or obstacles.

Art, design and architecture are also highly important for the human development. Friction is needed to keep the people intellectually awake, seduce people to think

とっても非常に重要です。摩擦は、人々を知的に目覚めさせ、人々に世界との関係について考えさせ、周囲の環境の意外な姿に直面することを可能にし、問題を提起し、社会の慣習に挑戦するために必要とされます。これは、アート・デザイン・建築の哲学的及び文化的機能です。摩擦のない世界では知性は衰え、摩擦のない芸術は単なる娯楽になります。

摩擦は「革新」と「創造性」の根源でもあり、アアルト大学創立時の私の思想において、これらは鍵となる2つの要素でした。アアルト大学は、21世紀の社会の構築に必要な教育と研究の環境を築くために、10年前に設立されました。アアルト大学では、科学と芸術、デザイン、ビジネス、テクノロジーといった分野を統合し、異なる思考間の「革新的な摩擦」が地球規模の課題に対して思いがけない解決策を生み出すことを可能にしました。私にとって、アアルト大学の重要な思想は「抜本的な創造性」であり、それは人々に「見えないものを見る」ことを促す知的環境です。

早稲田大学の渡邊大志准教授が制作した展覧会「Nation of Sorrow」は、視覚文化の重要性を強調し、デザイナーや建築家と熟練した職人のユニークなコラボレーションの価値を際立たせるなど、多くの点で重要です。展覧会では、ナショナル・アイデンティティを構築する上でのアート・デザイン・建築の役割についても分析し、私たちが誰であるか、何を表現するのかという2つの重要な論点に答えています。さらに、2つのデザイン立国である日本と

about their relationship to the world, enable facing surprising aspects in the environment, raise questions and challenge conventions. This is the philosophical and cultural function of art, design and architecture. World without friction would be intellectually dead, art without friction would be just entertainment.

Friction is also an important source of innovation and creativity, the two key ingredients of my idea of founding the Aalto University. Aalto was founded ten years ago to build an environment for education and research needed for building the 21st century society. Aalto brought together science and art, design, business and technology to enable "innovative friction" between the different ways of thinking for producing unforeseen solutions for the big global challenges. For me big idea of Aalto is "radical creativity", an intellectual environment, which will encourage and force the people "to see what they cannot see".

The exhibition "Nation of Sorrow" created by Associate Professor Taishi Watanabe, from Waseda University, Japan is important in many ways: it emphasizes the importance of the visual culture and highlights the value of the unique collaboration of designers and architects with highly skilled craftsmen. The exhibition also analyses the role of art, design and architecture in building the national identity, answering to two key questions: who we are, what do we stand for. The exhibition continues the long-lasting cultural dialogue of two design intensive nations, Japan and Finland, and tells of the role of The Japan Finland Design Association JFDA and The Finnish Institute of Japan in this dialogue. It is a continuation

フィンランドの長期にわたる文化的対話を
継続し、その対話のなかで日本フィンラン
ドデザイン協会 (JFDA) とフィンランドセ
ンターの役割について述べています。この
展覧会は、2003−2004年に東京でJFDA
とフィスカース社によって開催された
「Designing of Quietness」（静けさのデザ
イン）展の続編とも言えるものです。

to the "Designing of Quietness" exhibition by
JFDA in 2003-2004 in Tokyo and Fiskars.

Critique

建築は
無限ループである
Architecture is eternal loop

ペンティ・カレオヤ
建築家、アアルト大学・空間研究教授

Pentti KAREOJA,
Architect, Professor of Spatial Studies, Aalto University

　建築はゆっくりと進化しています。その様は、再び原初の状態に戻るまで、絶えず続く段階的な螺旋状のパターンに従っているようです。しかし、建築の旅は決して初期状態に戻ることはなく、旅先で何かが変化します。建築の様式は、同じことを繰り返すのではなく、旅の途中で新しい姿や層を獲得するからです。文化、技術、政治的価値観の変化は、ループする建築に新たな表現を再構築します。

　私が思うに、野心的で実験的な本建築展における渡邊さんの関心は、この建築の無

Architecture is slow evolution. It seems to follow constant and gradual spiral pattern until returning back to the very beginning, again. But it never returns back to the initial state, something changes during the trip. Architecture's mode is not identical repetition, but it gains new appearances and layers on the way. The changes in culture, technology and political values reformulate the returnee's newborn expression.

Taishi Watanabe's interests in his ambitious and experimental architectural exhibition, in my mind, are dealing with this eternal loop in architecture. The epicentre of

限ループの課題に取り組むことです。彼の見解の中心は、ナショナル・ロマンティシズムにあります。私の解釈では、渡邊さんの主なトピックは、様式としてのナショナル・ロマンティシズムの視覚的表現（フィンランドでは、アールヌーボーの解釈としてユーゲント・シュティールと呼ばれることがある）だけでなく、この表現の目に見えない次元を扱っています。渡邊さんは、「建築表現はどのように国のアイデンティティをもたらし、その普遍的性質を表現できるのか。今日の世界においてもナショナル・ロマンティシズムの価値観は有効であり、支持されているのか」と問いかけています。

建築の進化のなかで、永遠に変化する要素の１つは、自己表現との関係性です。その関係性は２極化されると思います。一方は、すべての感情を消去し、客観性を究極の理想とする合理的で普遍的な状態、他方は、見境のないほどに感傷的な状態です。驚くべきことに、ナショナル・ロマンティシズムは、必ずしも後者を代表するものではありません。実際に、明白な合理主義は、一見して想像できるよりも感傷的でロマンチックな表現をしている場合があります。同様に、ナショナル・ロマンティシズムは格段に分析的かつ合理的な側面を含むことがあります。

渡邊さんは、「哀しきネーション」と題されたこの展覧会で、日本とフィンランドのナショナル・アイデンティティの共通点を探し出し、その一貫した物語を構築しています。タイトルは、自然との強い関係性とともに、どこか寂しく、広大無辺な状態から成長する両国の基本的な特徴と結び付

his view is in national romanticism. My interpretation is that Taishi Watanabe's main topic is not only in the visual expression of national romanticism as a style (or jugend style as the interpretation of Art Nouveau is often named in Finland) but more in the invisible dimensions of this expression. Taishi asks: "how an architectural expression can deliver the nation's identity and express the common nature of it. Are the values of national romanticism still valid and endorsable into today's world"?

One eternally changing factor in architectural evolution is the relationship with the individual expression. It seems to be divided into two extremes, first the rational and universal mode where all the emotions are erased and objectivity is the ultimate ideal, and secondly the shameless sentimentality and individual expression. Surprisingly, the national romanticism is not necessarily representative of the latter. The apparent rationalism might in reality represent more sentimental and romantic expression than someone could imagine at first sight. In the same way national romanticism can contain predominantly analytical and rational dimensions.

Taishi Watanabe searches and finds common ground for Japanese and Finnish national identity and builds up a coherent narrative of it in this exhibition titled "Nation of Sorrow". The title seems to bind the both nations' basic characters which grow from certain melancholic and cosmic mood along with the strong relationship to the nature. Pragmatic attitude towards existence is shared attitude with the nations' basic character, yet there is space for mythical and religious aspects. In architecture and design the craftmanship and functionality are creating the plinth for the shared beauty.

いているようです。実在するものに対する即物的な考え方は、その国の基本的な特徴を共有していますが、神話的及び宗教的側面を含む余白があります。建築とデザインにおいては、職人技と機能性が両国に共有される美しさの基盤を築いています。

しかし、渡邊さんが問うように、ナショナル・ロマンティシズムの新しい解釈は、現代においてもまだ適切でしょうか。広く一般に共有されたプラットフォームから、局所的に同一視して理解できるデザインと建築の共通基盤を見つけることができるでしょうか。強力な反対勢力が存在するグローバリゼーションの時代には、ローカルアイデンティティを構築し、ゲニウス・ロキのかすかな領域を維持する必要があります。自然界のように、生物多様性も構築された環境のなかで栄え、強調されるべきです。おそらく、再認識されたナショナル・ロマンティシズムがその答えになるでしょう。

But is there still relevance for the new interpretation of national romanticism for today, as Taishi Watanabe questions? Could there be a common ground which allows the local identifiable interpretation in design and architecture from the same and universally shared platform? In the era of globalization there is a strong counterforce and need to build up the local identity and maintain the nuanced hierarchy of genius loci. As in the nature, the biodiversity should also bloom within the built environment and it should be emphasized. Perhaps reinvented national romanticism could be the answer.

Summary

縄文時代の縄、貝殻、そして魚の骨

Ropes, shells, and fish bones
in Jomon period

伏見 唯
Yui FUSHIMI

　例えば、ある２つの木材があったときに、それらを接合する方法を考えてみる。ガセット・プレートなどの金物でつなぎ留めたり、木を加工してつなぎ合わせるなどの複雑なやり方もあるが、単に２つの木材を「縄」で結んでつなぐという方法もある。

有り物の技術によるクリエーション

　日本の伝統的な木造建築の接合方法といえば、大工の職人技によって部材がつながるように木材を加工した、いわゆる「継手仕口」がすぐに思い起こされると思う。柱

　Consider, for example, how to join two pieces of wood together. There are more complicated methods, such as using gusset plates or other hardware or processing wood to join together. But there is also a simple method of tying two pieces of wood together with a rope.

To make things by versatile techniques

　When you think of the joining method of traditional Japanese wooden buildings, you might think of joint connection "Tsugite-Shiguchi" in which the wooden members are processed so that they are connected by

に四方から部材を取り付けた「四方差し」など、一見するとシンプルに部材が直交しているように見えるが、内部では実に複雑な仕掛けが施されて部材が接合されている。その妙技ゆえ、今でも日本のお家芸として世界に発信されているだろう (注1)。実際その歴史は長く、はるか原始の頃、鉄器を導入しはじめた日本の弥生時代では、人びとが暮らす素朴な竪穴式住居ですら、すでに一種の継手仕口で細部が納められていたと考えられ、復元されている (注2)。

しかしその前の新石器時代、日本の縄文時代においてはまだ青銅器や鉄器がなく、木材の加工技術にある程度の制限があったと想定され、この時代の遺跡においては、部材同士を縄や蔓で結んでつなげられた建築が復元されていることが多いのだ (注3)。丸太同士を縄でぐるぐる巻きにしてつなぐ。あるいは端部が2股に分かれたY字の自然木を利用して、うまく丸太を載せてから縄で縛る。継手仕口と比べれば、それ

the techniques of carpenters. At first glance, the members appear to be simply perpendicular to each other, as seen in the "four-way joint" in which four beams are attached to a single pillar from four sides, but inside the pillar, the beams and the pillar are joined by a very complicated mechanism. Because of this outstanding skill, it is probably still being known to the world as one of Japanese specialty[1]. In fact, the joint technique has a long history. Even during the Yayoi period in Japan, when ironware was first introduced, a kind of technique of joint connection is thought to have already been used in a primitive pit-house style and was restored[2].

However, during the Neolithic period and Jomon period in Japan before the Yayoi period, bronze and ironware were not yet made, and it is assumed that the technology of wood processing was not so advanced yet. For the ruins in the period, there were often restored dwellings which were made by tying the wooden members with ropes

登呂遺跡の接合部
Joint connection of Toro site

三内丸山遺跡の接合部
Joint connection of Sannai-Maruyama site

らはダイナミックで、いかにも原始的な姿に見える。

　原始的な姿というのは、いろいろと改良されていく前の姿。物と物をつなぐことを有り物で率直に実行した姿。建築の接合部のために生み出されたわけでもない汎用の材料（縄）を使い、接合への意志のみが現れたような姿になっている。継手仕口は、逆に建築の接合部のために改良を重ねた技術の粋であり、場所によって多様に使い分けながらも、接合の仕掛けなどないかのようにきれいに納められた姿が、縄とは対照的である。建築技術史の流れのなかでは、加工精度の向上により継手仕口が普及したことは接合技術の進展だと言わざるをえないが、縄による率直な姿にも惹かれる気持ちが芽生えないだろうか。

　縄は汎用の道具であるために、船を岸に結びつけたり、収穫した食物を吊して干しておいたり、様々な用途で活躍するが、いずれの場合でも元からの「有り物」である。カスタマイズの多寡はあれども、1つの用途のためだけに発明されたわけではない。ある用途のための改良をあまり感じず、「有り物」によって機能が満たされている姿は、多角的な効果を発揮しているというよりは、単一の目的のための実直な姿に思えるにちがいない。ただ、そのひたむきに目的に資するような姿が、むしろその用途の表象として昇華し、共感を生む意匠に化けうる可能性もあるのではないか。

周囲を取り巻く事物を刻印した土器

　そうした「有り物」が特徴的な意匠を生み出した例として、同じ縄文時代の土器がある。縄文時代の「縄文」という名称は、

and vines[3]. Logs are tied together in rope. Or, using a Y-shaped piece of natural wood with two ends, put a log on it and tie them with rope. Compared to joint fittings, they look crude and primitive.

Primitiveness is a figure before various improvements are made and also the one that frankly connects things with ordinary things around there. People used general-purpose material, such as rope, that was not produced just for connecting the members in building. It seems as if there appeared only a will to connect things. The joint connection is packed with the quintessence of techniques with the successive improvement of the connection part. In contrast to ropes, while various types of joint connections are used differently depending on the part of a building, they are neatly housed as if there is no connection mechanism. In terms of the history of architectural technology, it must be said that the popularization of the joint connection due to the improvement of processing accuracy is an advance in joining technology, but I wonder if the crude appearance of the joint by rope also attracts people.

Since the rope is a versatile tool, it is used for various purposes, such as tying ships to the shore, hanging and drying harvested food. In any case, people are using "ordinary things around there". The thing is not invented just for one use, though it is customized to different degrees. When little improvement has been made for some use, and the functions are fulfilled by "ordinary things around there", the tool must feel more honest for a single purpose than it has many effects. There is a possibility that the earnestness that concentrates on serving the purpose may be sublimated as

この時期の土器に施された縄の文様からきている。E.S. モースが、明治12（1878）年に行われた大森貝塚の考古学的な調査の報告書で、出土した土器の特徴として "the impression of well known cord mark" を挙げたためだという。代表的な文様は、撚った紐（縄）を回転しながら土器の表面に押し付けた文様である。なぜ縄だったのだろうか。

考古学者の可児通宏氏は、縄文について「装飾としての役割を否定しないまでも、同時に器面調整としての役目をも担っていたものと考えられる」と述べている (注4)。土器の製作工程のなかには、粘土によっておおよその全体の形ができあがった後に、表面の凹凸を均して平滑にしたり、細部の形を整える仕上げの作業があると考えられているが、その整形に縄などが用いられたという。つまり縄という汎用の道具をもって土器の表面を整えていたが、そうした目的が明白な作業の延長で、その道具と作業をまさに刻印するような縄文の装飾が施されたのだ。

縄のほかにも、食料などとして集落に持ち込まれた貝、魚、草などを土器の表面に当てて文様を写し取っていた。2枚貝や巻き貝を用いた貝殻文、食した魚の骨を押し付けた魚骨押捺文、回転させて押し付けた魚骨回転文などが知られている。自分たちの周囲を取り巻く日常的な諸物の刻印である。

これらは、いわば「有り物」による意匠ではないか。土器の装飾として独立して考案された意匠ではなく、他の目的、あるいは汎用の目的で周囲に元々存在していた物の現れであろう。その後の幾何学文様が際

a symbol of the use and transformed into a design that creates empathy.

An earthenware with an engraved mark on something surrounding it

The earthenware of Jomon period is an example of such a design created by "ordinary things around there". The name of "Jomon" came from the pattern of ropes applied to earthenware during this period. This is because E. S. Morse, an American zoologist and orientalist, pointed out "the impression of well-known cord mark" as a characteristic of the excavated earthenware in a report of the archaeological investigation of Omori Shell Mounds in 1878. The typical pattern of the earthenware is a twisted cord (rope) pressed onto the surface of earthenware while rotating. Why was a rope used?

Michihiro KANI, an archaeologist, thinks that the pattern of rope had played a role in adjusting the surface of the pottery, though he doesn't deny its decorative role[4]. It is thought that, in the process of making earthenware, after the overall shape was formed by clay, the surface of the earthenware was leveled to make it smooth, and the shape of the details was adjusted. The rope is said to be used to adjust its shape. In other words, the surface of the earthenware was arranged with a general-purpose tool, a rope, and this purpose was an extension of the fundamental function, and the decorations of rope were applied to the earthenware so as to mark the tool and the work.

In addition to ropes, patterns were copied by placing shellfish, fish, and grass brought to villages as food on the surface of earthenware. There are well-known patterns such as the shell pattern using bivalves and

立った弥生時代の土器においては、形を抽象化することで表現の幅が広がった展開を見せているが、その時代や地域の社会が率直に刻印されたような縄文時代の土器の表現も淘汰された過去のものというよりは、今でも見るべきものであると考えたい。

専門化による閉塞を打破するため原始に注目する

　原始に遡ってまで、こうした「有り物」が生み出す表現に注目しているのは、事物が歴史のなかで展開していくときに、次々と改良や淘汰を経て専門化が進んでいく一方で、その専門性に包括されない事物のあり方の可能性を言及したいためである。特に建築をはじめ、否応なく総合的な効果を発揮していくことになる事物の創造においては、その総合性ゆえの複雑な絡み合いを解決すべく、高度な技術や表現の体系が築き上げられていくだろう。例えば継手仕口も、部材を接合するという本来の目的意識のほかに、少なくとも取り合いをすっきりと納めようとする意志も働いているものだと思う。建築全体を見れば、耐久性、居住性、生産性、意匠性などのあまりにも多くの効果が期待されている創作物であり、その調停による総合性は簡単には獲得できるものではなく、積年の暗黙知の混入も多分に含まれているはずで、重視すべき専門化であることに疑いはない。

　それを踏まえながらも、本展が問題視しているような「専門化による閉塞」を打破しようとするならば、専門化がそれほど進む前のクリエーションのあり方に注目することも、選択肢の１つなのではないだろうか。例えば汎用の道具や周囲の日常的な

spiral shell, the fishbone seal pattern pressing the bones of the fish they ate, and the fishbone rotation pattern pressing the fish bones by rotating them. It is an engraving of everyday things around them.

These are, so to speak, the design based on "ordinary things around there". It is not a design devised independently as a decoration of earthenware, but a representation of things that originally existed around the earthenware for others or general purposes. In the earthenware with prominent geometric patterns in Yayoi period, the abstraction of the shape expanded the range of expression, but the expression of the earthenware in Jomon period, in which the society of the period or region was directly engraved, should still be seen today, rather than being regarded as a thing of the past that was eliminated.

Pay attention to the primitiveness to break the bottleneck of specialization

The reason why I pay attention to the expression produced by such "ordinary things around there" is to mention the possibility of the ideal way of things which are not included in the specialization, while the specialization advances one after another through improvement and selection as things develop in the history. Especially in the creative things that inevitably make a comprehensive effect, such as architecture, advanced technology and systems of expression will be established to solve the complicated intertwining things due to its comprehensiveness. For example, the joint connection has the original purpose of joining the members, but at least the intention to neatly handle each other would also exist in the improvement of the joint works. Taking the architecture from a wide

諸物を用いた「有り物」による意匠である。世界が変化を求めているとしたら、同じ人類の始原こそ、変化を待つ先駆者ともなりうるのではないだろうか。

perspective, architecture is a thing that is expected to have a great deal of effect in terms of durability, livability, productivity, and design, etc., and it is not easy to obtain a comprehensive property, and it must contain a lot of tacit knowledge for many years. So, there is no doubt that the specialization should be emphasized.

With that in mind, if we are going to break through the "specialization blockage" that this exhibition raises as a problem, then it may be an option to pay attention to the way creative activities used to be before they become so specialized. For example, it is a design by "ordinary things around there" using general tools and daily things. If the world is seeking change, the very beginning of the human race could be a pioneer waiting for change.

■注釈

注1 継手仕口による木組を含めた日本の伝統構法をユネスコ無形文化遺産にしようとする運動がある。継手仕口についての近年のまとまった書籍に、『木組 分解してみました』(竹中大工道具館、2019年、同名の企画展の図録)などがある。

注2 登呂遺跡、吉野ヶ里遺跡など。登呂遺跡を復元した建築史家・関野克は「出土木工品の精巧さからみて仕口も相当の程度発達していたと思われる」としている(関野克「登呂遺跡と建築史の反省」『建築雑誌』1947年10月号、日本建築学会)。

注3 三内丸山遺跡、根古谷台遺跡など。ただし、縄文時代の桜町遺跡にて貫や仕口の跡がある部材が出土し、ある程度継手仕口があったものとして、縄文時代の加工技術の見直しもなされている(『桜町遺跡シンポジウム：考古資料から建築材・建築技術を考える』桜町遺跡発掘調査団、2005年など)。

注4 可児通宏『縄文土器の技法』、同成社、2005年

■ NOTES

1. There is a movement to make Japanese traditional construction methods including wooden frames with joint connection inscribed on UNESCO intangible cultural heritage. One of the recently published books on joint connection is "KIGUMI: Revealing the Carpentry Behind the Wood Joint " published by Takenaka Carpentry Tools Museum on 2019, which is also published as pictorial records of the exhibition of the same title.

2. Toro Archaeological site, Yoshinogari site, etc. "Judging from the exquisite workmanship of the unearthed woodwork, it is considered that the accuracy of the joint connection was developed considerably". pointed out Masaru SEKINO, an architectural historian who restored Toro Archaeological site. (Masaru SEKINO. October, 1947. "Toroiseki to kenchikushi no hansei ". JOURNAL OF ARCHITECTURE AND BUILDING SCIENCE)

3. Sannai-Maruyama site, Negoyadai site, etc. However, wooden members with marks of Nuki, a tie beam penetrating pillar, and Shiguchi, a joint connection, were excavated at Sakuramachi site in the Jomon period, and this discovery has led to a review of the existence of wooden processing techniques even in Jomon period. (Sakuramachi site research project. Sakuramachi site symposium : Koukoshiryo kara kenchikuzai kenchikugijutsu wo kangaeru. 2005. etc.)

4. Michihiro KANI. Jomon doki no giho. Tokyo: Douseisha, 2005.

Greetings

我が友、渡邊大志さんがフィンランドで展覧会を開催することとなった。彼は、元々建築家で、今現在はサバティカルを活用して、日本の名門、早稲田大学からフィンランドのアアルト大学に留学中のところ、ここヘルシンキでその研究成果を披露してくれると聞き、大変楽しみにしてきたところである。

フィンランドのなかでも特にヘルシンキは、現代から近未来に至るデザインに優れた街で、Oodi や国立博物館にとどまらず、至る所、北欧の突き抜けるように爽やかで持続可能性を感じさせるデザインに一種の憧れを抱く人は世界中に数多く存在する。フィンランドにおけるデザインは、物静かである一方、内面の充実を確実に力強く世に示すための手段としてなくてはならない必然のものであり、それに触れた人に強烈なインパクトをもたらすものである。地政学的な困難さを持ち、それでいて平和を希求するフィンランドの人たちが無言のうちに、そうではない世の中に自分たちの願いを訴える力として大きな意義を有するものである。それは、自然との共生を人生の1つの大きなテーマとするフィンランドの人たちに深く根ざした力の源泉あるいは力の表象として生まれてくるもので、一見無機

My friend, architect, associate professor WATANABE Taishi, holds his first exhibition here in Helsinki. Taishi teaches at one of the prestigious universities in Japan, Waseda, and he has made use of his sabbatical by working as a resident researcher at Aalto University. I am so excited and looking forward to see his exhibition in which he entertains us with what he has learnt and experienced during his days in Finland.

It goes without saying that in Finland, Helsinki in particular, we are surrounded by the structures with superb design from modern to futuristic, such as; the National Museum and the Central Library, Oodi to name a few. Many across the globe cannot help but feel a sort of yearning for the Nordic style that is not only invigorating but also sustainable for many years to come. Finnish design, I personally believe, represents calmness, but at the same time, is inevitable as a means of expressing inner-fulfillment, thereby bringing eye-opening impact on those who have a chance to feel it. I interpret it as the power of silent appeal with great significance; the appeal of Finnish people who live in extremely difficult geopolitical surroundings, and yet wish to live peacefully in the world which unfortunately is not so tranquil. I can also see Finnish design as a source or symbol of power deeply enrooted within the soul of Finnish people who live

質に見えるが、実はそうではなく大変なエネルギーを内包した熱い魂のほとばしりを感ずるところである。

　ところで今年は延期され，来年には開催されるであろう東京オリンピックのモットーは United by Emotion である。アスリートたちが観客に興奮を与え、逆に観客から勇気づけられるように、見る人から発せられるエネルギーがまた建築家の想像力を掻き立てることにつながるのだろう。今回の展覧会で渡邊さんの示すデザインの魅力に引きつけられる人が多く出てくることを大いに期待している。

駐フィンランド特命全権大使
村田 隆

with a major theme of life in harmony with the great nature. It sometimes looks too monotonous and simple at first glance; on the contrary, I feel it shows a very lively passion imbued with unfathomable energy.

　"Incidentally" it is United by Emotion; the words that were revealed as motto for the Olympic and Paralympic Games in Tokyo, which have been postponed but will be held in the future. As athletes excite spectators and spectators encourage athletes, the energy generated from the audience would also stimulate the architect's imagination. I truly expect Taishi's works will attract as many people at the exhibition as possible.

Takashi MURATA
Ambassador Extraordinary and Plenipotentiary to Finland

この原稿は当初の展覧会開催予定に合わせて 2020 年 5 月に執筆いただいたものです。
This message was written in May 2020 in line with the original exhibition schedule.

3

Exhibitions

2 Japanese Crossover-Architecture

ユニティ・アーキテクチュア／理論編
ベルリン展

Unity Architecture / Theory Edition
Exhibition in Berlin

JAPANESE

@Technischen Universität Berlin

CROSSOVER-

Conceived and curated by Taishi WATANABE

ARCHITECTURE

ベルリン展カタログ表紙
Catalog Cover for the Exhibition in Berlin

　ベルリンでの「Japanese Crossover-Architecture」
展の扉絵はあえて文字だけとし、ビジュアルは用いな
いものとしました。そこには、「Nation of Sorrow」
展で発見したものを、可能な限り客観的に言語化し
た理論を提示したいという意思が込められています。
　Crossover する建築が持つ意味と可能性は、ヨル
ク・グライター教授が見事に理論として言語化して
くれています。異なる背景を持った多様な個人が共
有することができて初めてデザインの美しさは理論
となります。

On the cover art in the catalogue of the "Japanese
Crossover-Architecture" exhibition in Berlin, we used only
letters on purpose, so there are no images on it. In this
design, there is a will to present the things we found in the
"Nation of Sorrow" exhibition, as verbalized way
objectively as possible.

The meanings and the possibilities of crossovering
architecture is verbalized brilliantly as the theory by Prof.
Jörg Gleiter. When the diverse individuals who have the
different backgrounds can share ideas, the beauty of
designs becomes a theory.

Introduction

「Crossover-architecture」の論理
Logic of "Crossover-architecture"

渡邊大志
Taishi WATANABE

　ベルリンでの展覧会は「crossover-architecture」という建築理論を提唱し、その視点から日本の近現代建築のいくつかを紹介するものです。

　その目的は、20世紀の近代様式として整理された建築の概念とその具体的デザイン言語を今一度解体し、より継続的な建築と人間の関係からデザイン分野の別のない空間の理論構築を図ることにあります。

　建築は元来モニュメンタルなものです。衣食住とよく言われるように建築は文化で

The exhibition in Berlin advocates an architectural theory called "crossover-architecture" and introduces modern and contemporary Japanese architecture from this viewpoint.

This exhibition's purpose is to dismantle the commonly accepted architectural concept and its specific design language, which were categorized as the modern style of the twentieth century. Another purpose of this exhibition is building a theory of space that is distinct from the field of design by accounting for the more continuous relationship between architecture and

ある以前に文明であり、有史以来私たちが生き延びるために必要とする根源的なものの1つです。そのため建築を人間の歴史と切り離して捉えることは不可能であり、しかも往々にして建築の物理的寿命は個々の人間の寿命よりもはるかに長いものです。しかしながら、19世紀後半から20世紀前半にかけて様式主義から離陸すべくモダニズムの考えが提唱されていくなかで、歴史主義的表現からの離脱と実際の人間の歴史からの離脱が混同して理解されてしまったという問題があると思います。そのため、モダニズムの世界において建築が持つモニュメンタリティはある固定された時間の凍結された意思表示と曲解されてしまいました。必然的にその時間スパンは極めて刹那的であり、今日の建築デザインに対する社会的価値を押し留めている静圧は専らそのモニュメンタリティへの曲解によってもたらされていると考えます。

　確かにポストモダンの一連の試みは、この問題に気がついた一部の人々の間で共有された時代趣向とみることができます。しかし過去の歴史様式からその時代における意味を剥ぎ取った象徴的造形をコラージュし、アッセンブルするというその手法は、造形自体は何も更新されないという自らのデザインへの束縛となり、このことは皮肉的批評性を基盤とした辛辣な存在へと建築を貶めることにつながってしまいました。もし今、建築を専門としない多くの人たちに建築を自分から距離のある遠い存在だという認識があるとすれば、それはこの影響の大きさの証左と言えます。

　しかしながら、建築は1人の人間よりもはるかに長い時間を生きる存在であり、

humans.

　Architecture is monumental in nature. As is often referred to regarding food, clothing, and shelter, architecture is also a civilization before it is a culture; furthermore, architecture is one of the fundamental necessities we need for survival, and has been since the beginning of recorded history. Thus, it is impossible to separate architecture from human history, and the lifespan of architectural structure is often much longer than that of individual people. However, from the latter half of the nineteenth century to the first half of the twentieth century (when modernism was advocated to replace formalism) the separation of actual human history from the expression of historicism was confused. As such, the monumentality of architecture in modernism is misunderstood as a fixed expression from a particular time. Inevitably, any period of time is extremely ephemeral; thus, I believe that the static pressure that encapsulates the social value of today's architectural designs is derived solely from the exaggerated distortion of its monumentality.

　Indeed, a series of post-modern attempts can be seen as constituting a common epoch among those who have acknowledged the problem. However, the post-modernist method of collaging and assembling the symbolic form (which stripped the period's meaning from the historical form of the past) became a constraint on the designs of post-modernists in that the form itself was not renewed, which thus depreciates architecture and leads to a bitter existence formed from cynical criticism. If those who do not specialize in architecture think that

かつ、人間の歴史に絶えず寄り添わねば存在できないものです。そのため、建築の本来のモニュメンタリティは特定の象徴的造形によってもたらされるものではなく、常に建築を見て体験する人間の側にあるものであり、しかも同一の建築に対してそれは常に更新されるものです。

コンピュータによって格段にインタラクティブなサーフェイスに対面する機会が増した現代の人間にとって、これからの建築デザインにはより一層多くのモニュメンタリティを更新可能とする十分な「空白」（仮託する意味の余白）の担保の仕方が求められ、その方法が結果的に視覚芸術としての建築表現として私たちの生活空間のなかに立ち現れるでしょう。

その私たちの生活空間の原点を想像してみれば、初めは人間が生み出した生活のための工夫＝デザインに分野という概念はなかったはずです。有史以来の長い歴史のなかで膨大な人々による膨大なデザインがアーカイブされていくにつれて、それを便宜的に整理する方法や効率よくその技術の伝承を行う方法として分野という類型化の方法が合理的であったということに過ぎません。そして、分野は技術の類型とほぼ同じでしたから、本来であれば１つのデザインは織物、絵画、陶芸、彫刻、建築、映像といった複数の技術体系を自由に渡り歩き、それらの複合体として現れるべきものです。もし分野（＝技術の類型）がデザインを規定するとなれば、本末転倒と言うべきは明らかです。

しかし21世紀の私たちには、主に20世紀に作り上げた分野という概念を用いて

architecture is distant from them, it largely results from the magnitude of this effect.

However, architecture exists far longer than any single human being, yet cannot exist unless it is constantly and closely linked to human history. Therefore, the original monumentality of architecture is not created by a specific symbolic form but is always deriving its significance by someone seeing and experiencing the architecture; architecture's monumentality is caonstantly updated, even for the same architecture.

For people today, who now have increasing opportunities to face extremely interactive surfaces with computers, the future design of architecture will require a sufficiently innovative method of securing "blank" (i.e., a space used to represent something else) that will enable us to update more monuments. Furthermore, this method will eventually emerge in our living spaces in the form of architectural expression as visual art.

If we imagine the origin of our living spaces, originally there would not have been a concept of the "field" of design, which is an ingenuity created by humans for comfortable and useful living. As a significant number of designs have been created, and by many people and have been archived since recorded history, a method of categorization was the only rational way to classify them conveniently and to pass on each design's techniques efficiently. Because the concept of "field" is nearly synonymous with the type of technology, a design should be considered a complex of multiple technological systems, such as textiles, paintings, ceramics, sculptures, architecture, and images. If it is a field (i.e., a type of technology) that

物事を整理し、把握することに慣れ過ぎてしまいました。そのため、今の私たちが理解し易いようにデザイン本来の有り様を分野という概念の側からあべこべに捉えてみれば、その状態は crossover–media と形容することができます。ここで言う media とは、各分野の技術がアウトプットされる形式のことを指しています。要するに、分野がないという状態は相対的には分野横断と見えるわけです。

さらに、建築という即物的なアウトプットに限定してこのことを見てみれば、「建築が真に総合芸術であるためには、建築以外の分野のデザインによってのみ建築は構成される」という１つの論理が浮かび上がってきます。つまり、建築を見るとき、そこにはあらゆる分野のなかで唯一建築だけが不在であるという状態です。

本展覧会では、この建築に限定された crossover–media の状態を指して「crossover–architecture」と呼ぶことにしました。

冒頭で述べたように建築は元来モニュメンタルなものですが、この論理からすれば crossover–architecture のモニュメンタリティは常に技術を介してやってくることになります。建築という分野がないことは、建築という技術がないことと同じ原理だからです。つまり、分野が存在しない世界での建築にとって、技術は常に他分野（別の技術の類型）からやってくるしかありません。その技術は本来他の目的に用いるものでしたので、その適用がある程度終了した後におそらく一番最後に建築にやってくることでしょう。20 世紀における造船や飛行機を作る技術、昨今ではプロジェクショ

dictates the design, this is clearly putting the cart before the horse.

However, for us in the twenty-first century, we are too accustomed to organizing and understanding things within the concept of fields that were established mainly in the twentieth century. Therefore, to make design understood easily, if we review what design should be from the perspective of the concept of a field in a retrograde way, then we can describe the state as "crossover-media". In this context, "media" is defined as the format within which the technology of each field is an output. In short, a field's absence is, relatively speaking, a state of crossing over between diverse fields.

Furthermore, when we consider this idea in terms of architecture's tangible output, the following logic emerges: in order for architecture to be truly a comprehensive art, it must consist of designs from fields other than architecture. In other words, architecture does not contain only the field of architecture among various fields.

In this exhibition, a logic of "crossover-media" limited to architecture is defined as a logic of "crossover-architecture".

As I mentioned earlier, architecture is monumental in nature, but from this logic, the monumentality of "crossover-architecture" always comes through technology. This is so because the absence of the field of architecture operates by the same principle as the absence of architectural technology. In other words, because architecture does not have a field of architecture itself, architectural technology must always derive from another field (i.e., another type of technology). Originally, the specific technology used was intended for purposes other than architecture, so it is probably incorporated into architecture later.

ンマッピングやVRの技術などはそのわかり易い例です。ただ、ここではそれよりももう少し身近でスケールの小さい些細な技術について取り上げたいと思います。

そのようなcrossover-architectureにおいて、モニュメンタリティの空白を作るということは技術＝分野の空白を意図的に生み出すということです。これを逆に見れば、モニュメンタリティの更新は新たにやってくる技術＝分野の価値観によってももたらされることになります。

これらのことから、crossover-architectureを以下のように定義することができます。

1. デザインや生産が建築以外の分野（＝技術）の方法を含む、あるいは建築以外の分野の方法に及ぶ
2. 設計者（建築家）と施工者（職人）に別れない製作過程を持つ
3. 結果として、壁、床スラブ、柱、窓といった建築部位をデザインがまたぐ（デザインの部位と機能の部位の枠組みが一致しない）

その上で本展では、日本最古の現存する木造建築物である法隆寺五重塔（6世紀）に用いられた鍛造釘を復元し、これを上記に定義したcrossover-architectureの具体的なマイルストーンとしました。

これらの鍛造釘は古代における木造の超高層ビルを実現するために作られたものです。その製作に当時の刀剣や祭具などを作っていた鍛冶職人が従事したことは想像に難くありません。木工大工による木組みで構造体は作られていますが、地震の多い日本では外側から見えないようにこれらの

Examples include technologies used for building ships and airplanes in the twentieth century, projection mapping, and Virtual Reality (VR) technologies today. However, here, I would like to cover a smaller and more familiar technology.

In crossover-architecture, creating a void of monumentality means intentionally creating a void of technology (fields). From the opposite perspective, the renewal of monumentality emerges from the values of new technologies (fields).

Based on this line of reasoning, the phase, "crossover-architecture", is defined as follows:

1. Covering or involving methods in fields (i.e., technologies) other than architecture in design or production.
2. Having a manufacturing process that does not separate designers (i.e., architects) and builders (craftsmen).
3. As a result, the structure's design covers the parts of the building, such as the walls, floor slabs, columns, and windows (the design of the structure's framework does not match the framework's functions).

In this exhibition, we restored forged nails used in the five-story pagoda of the Horyuji Temple, which was built in the sixth century (and is Japan's oldest existing wooden building). Additionally, we used the forged nail as a concrete milestone for the term "crossover-architecture".

These forged nails were made for constructing the pagoda's ancient wooden skyscraper. It is easy to imagine that the same blacksmiths who made swords and ritual tools also produced these nails. The skyscraper itself is made of wood and

鍛造釘が仕込まれたのでしょう。それらは隠し釘で見た目には見えないため、1500年ほどの時を経た現在では五重塔には「日本最古の木造建造物」というモニュメンタリティが託されています。しかし、当時のそれは伝来したばかりの仏教の先進性を表す最先端技術でしたし、現代になってこの鍛造釘の存在を知れば、五重塔にはまた違った価値感によるモニュメンタリティが与えられるでしょう。そこで、本展覧会ではこの五重塔に crossover-architecture というモニュメンタリティを託したいと考えました。

　具体的にはこのようにして、分野すなわち技術の付与が別のモニュメンタリティを新たに付与することにつながります。その他の展示物においても五重塔と同様に、「建築以外によってもたらされた建築」という crossover-architecture の視点で日本の近現代建築の技術的表象としてのデザインを切り抜き、提示しました。

　実際のところ、それらには「日本の」近現代建築の特殊性が表れていると言えます。

　約150年前、欧米諸国から文明文化を輸入することによって日本は近代化を遂げました。建築はその代表的なものの1つでした。それまで建築という分野が存在しなかった日本には、建築という名の技術もありませんでした。当初日本の近代建築は、木工大工の他は建築以外の分野の職人を集めて作られました。擬洋風と呼ばれる西ヨーロッパの様式建築を木造でアレンジした建築はその際たるもので、それに類するデザインを総称して和魂洋才や和洋折衷と

constructed by carpenters, however, these forged nails were inserted in such a way that they could not be seen from outside. Because the nails are hidden, the five-storied pagoda is now entrusted with the monumentality of being "Japan's oldest wooden structure" after fifteen hundred years. However, simultaneously, the structure included the most advanced technology that represented the progressiveness of Buddhism, which was introduced in Japan at the same time. As such, if we know about this forged nail in our own time, then this five-storied pagoda will be lent a sense of monumentality and a significant sense of value. Therefore, in this exhibition, this five-storied pagoda is presented in the context of its monumentality, which we call "crossover-architecture".

In this way, the addition of another field or technology (such as forged nails) creates that sense of monumentality. Similarly to the five-story pagoda, other exhibits show that the design of modern and contemporary Japanese architecture was cut out and presented as a technical representation from the perspective of "crossover-architecture", or as "architecture brought about by something other than architecture".

In fact, the peculiarity of "Japanese" modern architecture is expressed in the exhibitions. Approximately 150 years ago, Japan modernized itself by importing civilized culture from Western countries; architecture is one such example. At that time, a distinct field of architecture, as well as the technology called architecture, had not yet been recognized. In those days, Japan's industry of modern architecture was started by a group of craftsmen other than carpenters. A typical example is pseudo-

呼びます。つまり、基本的に日本の近現代建築はその延長にあると言え、この問題は日本の建築家たちにとって長年の課題でもありました。そこで本展では、それらを和洋折衷ではなく、他分野による建築として見直すことで、その建築的な可能性をcrossover-architectureとしてヨーロッパや世界の人たちと共有する方法を意図しました。ですので、どの国や地域出身のみなさんにも、それぞれが生まれ育ってきた環境になぞらえながら日本という他国で出力された異なる手法と表現を普遍的な眼でもって観察していただきたく思います。

　加えて、ここにある展示物はそれ自体が1つのcrossover-architectureの状態を示すと同時に、それらが1つひとつの断片として展示空間そのものをcrossover-architectureとすることも意識しています。それは、本展覧会が過去の遺物の再解釈ではなく、未来に来たるべき空間を生む論理であるためです。いずれ、実際の建築としてもお目にかけることができると思います。

　ここに陳列する展示物たちを、日本にある実際の物をプリントしたコピーや情報ではなく、会場にcrossover-architectureを空間化する本物のマテリアルとして眺めていただければ幸いです。

Western-style (Giyo-fu) architecture, which resembled Western-style construction but relied on the techniques of traditional Japanese wooden architecture. As such, the designs similar to Giyo-fu are collectively called "Japanese spirit with Western technology" (Wakon-yosai) or "harmonization of Japanese and Western style" (Wayo-secchu). In other words, Japanese modern and contemporary architecture is essentially an extension of these styles, and has been a long-standing problem for Japanese architects. Therefore, in this exhibition, by reviewing the peculiarity not as a mixture of Japanese and Western styles, but as architecture in other fields, we intend to share the architectural potential with Europe, and with the world, as "crossover-architecture". I aspire for people worldwide to observe the different architectural methods and expressions produced in other countries (such as Japan) and compare them to their own environments in which they were born and raised, yet also doing so from a universal perspective.

In addition, the exhibits themselves show the state of a "crossover-architecture"; simultaneously, the exhibits are intended to make the exhibition space itself an example of "crossover-architecture", piece-by-piece. This is because this exhibition is not a reinterpretation of relics from the past but is itself a logic that creates a space for the future: such an actual building will itself be constructed in the future.

I hope that the individual exhibits displayed here will be viewed not as copies or information printed from actual objects in Japan, but as tangible materials that embody the concept of "crossover-architecture".

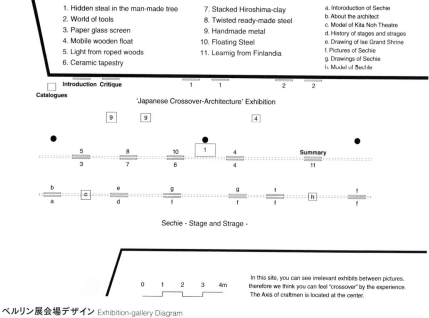

1. Hidden steal in the man-made tree
2. World of tools
3. Paper glass screen
4. Mobile wooden float
5. Light from roped woods
6. Ceramic tapestry

7. Stacked Hiroshima-clay
8. Twisted ready-made steel
9. Handmade metal
10. Floating Steel
11. Learnig from Finlandia

a. Intoroduction of Sechie
b. About the architect
c. Model of Kita Noh Theatre
d. History of stages and strages
e. Drawing of Ise Grand Shrine
f. Pictures of Sechie
g. Drawings of Sechie
h. Model of Sechie

Catalogues   Introduction Critique   1   1   2   2

'Japanese Crossover-Architecture' Exhibition

9   9   4

5   8   10   1   4   Summary
3   7   6   4   11

b   c   e   g   g   f   h   f
a   d   f   f   f   f

Sechie - Stage and Strage -

0 1 2 3 4m

In this site, you can see irrelevant exhibits between pictures.
therefore we think you can feel "crossover" by the experience.
The Axis of craftmen is located at the center.

ベルリン展会場デザイン Exhibition-gallery Diagram
ベルリン工科大学／ホワイエ・ギャラリー Foyer-Galerie, Technische Universität Berlin

新しいモニュメンタリティと デジタルのドキュメンタリティ

New monumentality and digital documentality

ヨルク・グライター
建築家、ベルリン工科大学建築理論学教授

Jörg H. GLEITER
Architect, Professor of Architectural Theory
at the Technische Universität Berlin

世界は絶え間なく変化しているという一般的な認識に反して、"Japanese Crossover-Architecture" 展は、人間と建築の永続的で欺瞞なき関係に焦点を当てています。建築は人間が生き残るために必要なツールであると主張することで、建築の人類学的な礎に迫るものです。ウィトルウィウスは既にこのことを指摘しながらも、同様に建築のみならず言語と共同体も建築と対等な立場の２つのツールであるとしました。人間は言語を学んで初めて共同体を形成し、共同体が基盤となって小屋を建てたのです。

Contrary to the general perception that the world is in a state of constant change, the exhibition Crossover-Architecture focuses on the permanence and non-negotiability of the relationship between man and architecture. It addresses the anthropological foundation of architecture by arguing that architecture is one of the tools without which man cannot survive. Vitruvius had already pointed this out, but he also mentioned two other tools that he placed on an equal footing with architecture: language and community. For as he tells us, people first had to learn language to form

しかし、人類学的な礎について語る時、建築、言語、共同体の関係性が常に不変であるということではありません。むしろ逆に、ツールとしての建築は変化しますが、そこでも建築そのものと人類への使命に対してどれだけ真正であり続けられるのか、という問いが生じるものです。

コペルニクス的転回

今日、建築の人類学的な礎について考える場合、人工知能とそれがもたらす建築への影響に焦点を当てなければなりません。それはこの最新技術の合理性の故にではなく、人類学的次元の故に、さらに人間の自己理解に対して人工知能が及ぼす変化の故にです。なぜなら、これまで人間をその他から峻別するものであった特殊性が、AIの登場によって、人間固有のものではなくなるからです。それは創造性です。ご存知のとおり、人工知能は人間の創造性とどんどん競い合うようになってきました。ここで起きていることは、単に劇的な変化以上のものです。まさに、長い人類史における4度目のコペルニクス的転回とも呼ぶべき現象が生じようとしています。

最初のコペルニクス的転回は、天文学者ニコラウス・コペルニクス（1473-1543）によって引き起されました。太陽系、天体、惑星が地球の周りを回っているのではなく、地球が太陽の周りを回っていることを彼は示しました。地動説により、人類は宇宙の中心であるというそれまでの立場を失い、地球と共に人類の位置も周縁へと移動しました。2度目のコペルニクス的転回は、チャールズ・ダーウィン（1809-82）によるものです。人間は神が創造したために

human communities, which in turn is the basis and purpose for building shelter. However, when one speaks of anthropological foundations, this does not mean that the relationship between architecture, language, and community always remains unvaried. On the contrary, the question arises of how architecture can remain true to itself and its anthropological mission precisely through change.

Copernican Revolution

If we inquire into the anthropological foundations of architecture today, our focus must be on artificial intelligence and its influence on architecture. Not because of a fascination for the advanced technology, but because of the changes it triggers in human self-understanding. Because with AI the last thing that distinguishes a human being as unique from others falls: creativity. One simply has to acknowledge that artificial intelligence is increasingly competing with human creativity. There is no doubt that what is happening here is more than dramatic. What is emerging is what in the long history of mankind must be called nothing less than the fourth Copernican turning point.

The first Copernican revolution was triggered by the astronomer Nicolaus Copernicus (1473-1543), who was able to show that the solar system, the stars and planets, do not revolve around the earth, but the earth revolves around the sun. Thus, man lost his position in the center of the cosmos and together with the Earth, he moved into a marginal position. The second Copernican revolution is associated with Charles Darwin (1809-82), who recognized that mankind does not owe its uniqueness to being created by God, but that Man is related to the animal world from which he

唯一無二なのではなく、動物界に関連しており、進化の過程で生じたものであると認識しました。3度目のコペルニクス的転回は、ジークムント・フロイト（1856-1939）に始まります。フロイトの精神分析は、人間が自己の主体なのではなく、無意識、エス（イド）が自我の主であることを示し、啓蒙主義の信念を揺るがしました。コペルニクス的転回が起こるたびに、新しい科学的認識が人間の世界観を大きく震撼させてきたのです。

　そして人間は今、最後に残された創造の特権をコンピュータに対して失いつつあり、これをコンピュータと分かち合わなければなりません。このことは、人間の自己意識を傷つけるだけでなく、人類学上の人間の地位をめぐり、深刻な危機に至らせます。人間が科学や研究を通じて自己と世界について知れば知るほど、人類が中心から周縁に移動してしまうという矛盾が常にありました。それが今、人工知能にも当てはまるのです。マリオ・カルポのような一部の理論家はすでにこれを第2次デジタルターンであると宣言していますが、この発展はまだ始まったばかりです。本当の衝撃はこれからなのです。言語論的転回であれ現象論的転回であれ、これまで英語で「ターン」と称された転回なるものは、世界を単に読み替えてきただけです。しかしコペルニクス的転回は英語で「レボリューション」と定義される転回であり、人間の心理に深く入り込み、人間の意識と世界における立ち位置を変えてゆきます。

ビッグデータ：建築の新しい実体性

　一般的予測に反して、建築に及ぼす人工

evolved. The third Copernican revolution was initiated by Sigmund Freud (1856-1939). Freudian psychoanalysis shattered some Enlightenment convictions by showing that man is not master of himself, that the id, the unconscious, is master of the ego. With each Copernican revolution, new scientific knowledge deeply shook the world view of man.

And now man must share the privilege of creativity with the computer. This not only bothers man's self-consciousness, it leads to a profound crisis as far as the anthropological status of the human being is concerned. Though it is a paradox, the more man knows about himself and about the world through science, the more he moves from the center to the fringe. This now also applies to artificial intelligence. By the way, when we talk about the Copernican turn, it goes far beyond the talk of the digital turn, even if some theorists like Mario Carpo already announced the second digital turn. But the real shock is yet to come. These repeatedly proclaimed turns, such as the digital turn, the linguistic turn or the phenomenological turn only interpret the world differently. The Copernican revolutions, though, reach much deeper into the human psyche, they change the consciousness of man toward himself and his position in the world.

The New Materiality of Architecture

Unlike general expectations, the growing influence of artificial intelligence does not lead to a rupture within the concept of architecture, but, to make a concept by Fredric Jameson fruitful for the question of Big Data, it nonetheless leads to a momentous shift within the system of cultural dominants[1]. This brings us to the central

知能の影響力の高まりが、建築のコンセプト内に分断をもたらすことはないでしょう。しかし、ビッグデータをめぐるフレドリック・ジェイムソンの概念を用いてこれを先に進めるならば、それでもなおビッグデータは文化的支配体系内において、それに劣らぬ重大な変化を招き、多大な影響が生じることになります(注1)。そうして我々は、「建築における人工知能の影響が、モニュメンタリティからドキュメンタリティへの移行に現れる」という、この論文の主題に至るのです。ドキュメンタリティ(documentality)という用語は、イタリア人哲学者のマウリツィオ・フェラーリスに起因します(注2)。この哲学用語を建築に置き換えるならば、建築におけるドキュメンタリティは、建築固有の変化において生じます。その理由は、以下で考察するように、ビッグデータが建築における新しいマテリアルの基盤を形成するからです。

建築の再概念化においてマテリアルが持つ意味は、非常に一般的には日本の建築を例に説明することができます。例えば、世界最古の木造建築である奈良法隆寺の五重塔の建設に使用された最初の鍛造和釘が示すもので、これはピエール・ブルデューの社会学に関連性を持つ渡邊さんのフィールド理論を支えます。その理論とは、建築の革新において決定的な推進力は常に建築以外の分野から来るというものです。7世紀当時には、それが鍛造和釘でした。これを使用することで、当時としては卓越した大きさの五重塔を建立することができた訳ですが、それまで建築は木組技術に基づいていたので、和釘は建築の外の文化からやって来たということになります。さらに、釘

thesis: the influence of artificial intelligence in architecture manifests itself in the transition from the concept of *monumentality* to *documentality*. The term *documentality* goes back to the Italian philosopher Maurizio Ferraris[2]. Under reorientation of the contents that Ferraris identified for philosophy, documentality in architecture manifests itself in the specific change of architecture as a document. The reasons for this, as will be argued below, they lie in Big Data as the new materialistic basis of architecture.

In general, the significance of the material for the reconceptualization of architecture can be illustrated using an example from Japanese architecture. The wrought iron nails that were first used in the construction of the five-story pagoda of Horyuji in Nara -- the oldest wooden building in the world -- exemplify Watanabe's field theory, which is loosely related to the sociology of Pierre Bourdieu. It states that the decisive impetus for innovations in architecture always comes from a field other than architecture. In the 7th century it was the use of wrought-iron nails, which made it possible to build a five-story pagoda of dimensions unsurpassed at the time. One has to notice, though, that the nails belonged to a cultural field that had not been part of architecture as til then architecture was based on wood techniques. Furthermore, it is significant that the nails were applied invisibly. Had they remained visible, their visible presence would have intervened in the established system of meanings. New elements that one is unfamiliar with and that cannot be interpreted beyond their actual constructive function always cause great irritation.

For each new material and form, a semantic code must first emerge so that the

が見えないように使用されたことも重要です。もし釘が目に見えるままであったならば、その可視的存在が、それまでの意味の体系に干渉していたでしょう。その際、新たな要素として出てきた目に見える釘に、人々は本来釘の持つ機能以上の解釈を施すことはできなかったはずで、苛立ちを感じたことでしょう。

　従来のマテリアルやフォルムが、既存の言語文法内において新しいものに置き換わり、解釈されるためには、意味論上のコードが形成される必要があります。例えば、ジャック＝ジェルマン・スフロが設計したパリの「サント＝ジュヌヴィエーヴ修道院（1790）」のように、18世紀のヨーロッパ建築において、鉄は鉄筋の形で多用され、石造の構造体の引張力に代わってゆきます。この鉄筋は、法隆寺の鍛造和釘と同様、見えないように使用されていました。なぜなら、鉄筋は古典主義の言語に干渉してしまうからです。人々は目に見える鉄筋を解釈できず、物質的な存在以上の意味をそこに見出すこともできなかったでしょう。そして通常、理解できないものは美しくない、つまり醜悪であると感じられるものですから、この場合にも古典様式を醜く邪魔するものと捉えられてしまったことでしょう。

　このことは、建築を理解する上の基本となる視点です。マテリアルの基盤が、建築言語とその象徴的機能に変化をもたらすことを、上の例は示しています。それならば、今日の建築の前提条件の変化をめぐる問いも、そのように見なければなりません。西暦600年頃に奈良で伝統的に釘を用いない木組から鍛造和釘の利用へ移行したように、ビッグデータを背景にした我々は、マ

new can be given a place within the existing grammar of materials and forms. In 18th-century European architecture, iron was already used in many ways as reinforcement steel to take over the tensile forces in stone constructions, for example in the construction of S. Geneviève (1790) by Jacques-Germain Soufflot in Paris. Like the wrought-iron nails in Horyuji, this steel also remained invisible. It would have interfered with the language of classicism in a disturbing way. It could not have been interpreted or been given a higher meaning beyond its material appearance. If the steel elements had remained visible, the steel elements and subsequently the entire building would have been perceived as ugly, because usually what is not understood is called the opposite of beautiful, namely ugly.

In important aspect emerges that is fundamental to understanding architecture. Changes in the material basis lead to change in the language of architecture and its symbolic function. This is also where the question of the changing conditions for architecture today must begin. Against the background of Big Data, we need to broaden the concept of material, just as it was the case in the transition from the traditional wooden connection to the wrought-iron nail in Nara around the year 600. We need to recognize the new material basis for architecture in an age of Big Data. Doubtlessly, the new material of architecture today is the mass of data that is collected, analyzed, and in data-based design applied to architecture. Stone, wood, steel or aluminum are increasingly turned into a function of Big Data.

Monumentality

Is one of the central concepts of

テリアルの概念を広げる必要があります。ビッグデータに建築のための新たなマテリアル基盤を見る以上、マテリアル概念を広げなければなりません。収集、分析、評価された大量のデータが、データベースのデザインプロセスを通じて建築を形成してゆきます。それは、新たな建築のマテリアルなのです。石、木、スチール、アルミニウムは、段々とビッグデータの1機能になってゆくでしょう。

モニュメンタリティ

　モニュメンタリティは、建築の中心となる概念に数えられ、重要な建築技法の1つです。建築が物質的な存在を超越して、特にそこから非常に遠くにある事象や、そこにはない事象を呼び起こさせる力を与えるモニュメンタリティはまた、マテリアル性と意味の間に生じる緊張のなかに置かれています。マテリアルの記号を通じて建築は、そこにない、他の事象を示します。モニュメンタリティを通じた建築のマテリアル存在の超越化と言い換えることができるでしょう。パリの「サント＝ジュヌヴィエーヴ修道院」の例を再び用いるならば、この建造物は、柱、アーキトレーブ、クーポラ等の様式エレメントを用いることで、自身を超えて、古典古代とその当時の理想的価値観を示しているのです。それらは、建築マテリアルとしてここで用いられた石のなかに刻み込まれた記号です。

　モニュメンタリティによって、建築は自身より大きな何かを記録するものとなります。他の事象を指し示す、解読可能な記号が、マテリアル内に書き込まれていることがその特徴です。そのためモニュメンタリ

architecture as well as one of the most important architectural techniques. Monumentality is associated with the ability of architecture to refer beyond its material presence to ideas and things that are not present. By means of material signs, architecture is able to refer to things that are absent. Hence, monumentality consists of the tension between materiality and sign, between things present and absent. One could also speak of the transcendence of the material presence of architecture through monumentality. S. Geneviève in Paris can again serve as an example. By means of columns, architraves, capitals, and ornaments the building refers beyond itself to ancient times of antiquity and the ideal values that are associated with it. They are carved into the material of the architecture, here, into the stone.

By means of monumentality, architecture becomes a document of something larger than itself. Monumentality thus has something to do with signs and their legibility and with the fact that signs always need a material in which they can be inscribed. In semiotics this is called a *sign carrier*, which is needed for any sign to be legible and durable, whether paper or stone. One might object that there are also buildings that exhibit no or only few signs, buildings that perhaps have smooth, untreated facades free of ornamentation and images, such as the Pyramid of Khufu or the Pyramid of Cestius in Rome. Yet these buildings are not monumental in the true sense, they are simply very large but do not exhibit features of monumentality. They are characterized by what can be described as *bigness*.

Monumentality is revealed in the fact that the material presence of architecture is

ティは、記号と、その解読可能性、そしてその記号が書き込まれる先であるマテリアル存在の必要と関連しています。紙かもしれませんし、石かもしれません。しかしここで反論が出るでしょう。例えばクフ王のピラミッドやローマのケスティウスのピラミッドのように、記号を全くあるいはあまり持たず、平らで装飾を伴わず表面を処理していないファサードの建造物も見られると。しかし、これらの建造物はとても大きいだけで、本来の意味においてモニュメンタルではなく、むしろレム・コールハースが1990年代に定着させたビッグネスの定義によって描写すべきものです。

　建築のマテリアル的な存在が、不在の何かを参照する記号よって超越されることで、モニュメンタリティは顕在化されます。それにより建築は知性と想像力の媒体となり、このようにして芸術的かつ知的な行為となってゆきます。建造物が自己と物質的・物理的限界を超えて成長しているとも言えます。自己を超えた成長を通じ、建造物が建築となるのです。ここでいう自己を超えた成長とは、記号性が、強力な効果及び美学概念上の崇高性と結びつくことを意味しています。モニュメンタリティによって、建築は自己を超えて、拡張された思考と感覚的体験のスペースとなり、そのスペースには建築以外の文化的領域も含まれます。建築外の事象を参照することで、建築的物体が文化的力場に統合され、今度はその一部分として、効果を発揮するのです。

　今日の建築における新しさとは、記録の特性の変化にあり、また記録の特性をかなりの部分放棄してしまうことにあります。これは、コンピュータの容量の増加により、

transcended by the sign reference to something absent. In this way architecture becomes an intellectual medium and a medium of imagination; it opens itself up to artistic and intellectual endeavors. It can be said that the building grows beyond itself and its material-physical limitations. It can be said that the building thus outgrows itself and its material-physical limitations. Growing beyond oneself then means that the symbolic qualities are combined with strong effects and the aesthetic concept of the sublime. Thus, we can maintain that monumentality short-circuits two experiences: thinking and sensual experience. By means of monumentality, architecture grows beyond itself and becomes an expanded field of thought and experience. Through its reference to things outside architecture, the architectural object fits into the cultural force field of which it is a part and in which it develops its effect.

What is new in architecture today lies in its changed documentary character or even, at times, its renunciation. This has to do with the changing conditions of cultural production that results from the growing storage capacity of computers. However, it would be a mistake to assume that data-based design only concerns the material and structural data. Data based design today means that the design process is based on data about emotional, mental and physical states, expectations and desires. In addition to the technical data, these data become the basis of the design process. Big Data is not limited to the objective and quantifiable facts, but also records purchasing, consumption, and leisure time behavior, mental states, and emotional patterns. What unconsciously determines life can easily be analyzed by means of

文化的生産の条件が変化した事実と関係があります。しかしながら、データをベースとしたデザインが、建築デザイン、構造、生産それぞれを結びつけ、調整する助けとなるマテリアルのデータ、また構造上のあるいは構築上のデータのみに関係があると考えるのは間違いでしょう。昨今のデータをベースとしたデザインとは、感情・心理・身体の状態、期待、願望などについてのデータを基盤にデザインプロセスが生じることを意味しています。技術的な情報に加えてこれらのデータもデザインプロセスの基盤を形成します。ビッグデータは、客観的で定量化可能な事実に限定されず、購買、消費、余暇の行動、心理状態、さらには感情的な行動パターンまでも把握します。無意識のうちに生活を左右するものが、人工知能により分析され、建築家を後目にそれが建築物体のフォルムや形態のパラメーターとなるのです。

デジタル・ドキュメンタリティ

　モニュメンタリティとは対照的に、ドキュメンタリティが描写するのは、データは目に見える記号ではなく、もはやマテリアリティも持たない、ということです。データはコンピュータメモリのどこかにデジタルのバイナリコードとしてのみ存在するのですから。そのようなバイナリコードが、目に見えて解釈可能なフォルム、記号、装飾、イメージで溢れた隠喩などと異なる点は、バイナリコードは目に見えず何一つコミュニケートしないことです。バイナリコードは内容も歴史も持ちません。バイナリコードが目指すのは、ストーリーではなく効果であり、相互関連性がその前提とな

artificial intelligence and become a parameter of form and shape of the architectural object, bypassing the architect.

Digital Documentality

In contrast to monumentality, digital documentality describes the fact that data are not visible signs and no longer have any materiality, since they exist somewhere in the memories of computers only as digital, binary codes. It distinguishes the binary codes from the visible and interpretable forms, signs, ornaments and pictorial metaphors that they are invisible and therefore cannot express anything. They are not aimed at narrative, but at effect, which requires that they be linked to each other first. Only then is their actual purpose activated. This is what distinguishes digital documentality from monumentality: Digital documentality describes the renunciation of the documentary character of architecture and the shifting of the balance of the expanded field of thought and experience to the side of experience, and thus to the side of the effect.

The architectural objects of today are increasingly generated from a wealth of data, which are less concerned with meaning than with effect. Projects such as the King Power MahaNakhon Tower in Bangkok by Olé Scheren or the Provincial Headquarters in Antwerp by Xaver de Geyter aim to evoke admiration and strong emotions. They are no longer part of a grand narrative of architecture. They no longer want to explain or justify where they come from or what they refer to. They're just there, present. Projects like Bałtyk by MVRDV in the Polish city of Posnan are hermetically self-contained and rely solely on monumental effects. Style and ornaments

ります。そうして初めて、もともとの目的へと活用され、効果を発揮します。それがドキュメンタリティの特徴です。ドキュメンタリティは、建築の記録的な特性を殆ど放棄することを意味し、建築の拡張された思考と体験のスペース内におけるバランスを、経験のスペースへ、ひいては効果へとシフトしていくことを示しています。

今日の建築的物体の傾向は、豊富なデータから次々と生成されることにあり、それは意味ではなく効果を目指すものです。例えば、オーレ・シェーレンが設計したバンコクの「キングパワー・マハナコン・タワー」や、ザヴェール・デ・ヘイテル設計の「アントワープ行政区庁舎」は、驚嘆と強い感情を喚起することを目的としています。それらはもはや壮大な建築のナラティブの一部ではありません。どこから来て、何を参照するのかを説明し、実証したいわけではないのです。それらはただそこに建ち、存在しているだけです。ポーランドの街ポズナンでMVRDVが設計した「バルティック」は完全に自己完結しており、記念碑的な効果のみに頼っています。ナラティブは不在で、パターン技法が様式や装飾に取って代わり、また意味論的な知性の次元は情緒的効果に換えられています。建築家が持つ批判理論的かつ個人的な志向性は、ビッグデータに基づく集合的志向性により置き換えられるのです。

ドキュメンタリティによる建築は、実はフリードリヒ・ニーチェの「偉大な様式」思想とも関連しているため、歴史的な前例が無いわけではありません。彼は建築を「どんな証明も必要とせず、喜ばすことを拒絶し、軽率に答えず、（中略）宿命的に法の

are replaced by a technique of pattern, and the semantic, intellectual dimension is replaced by emotional impact. The critical-individual intentionality of the architect is substituted by a collective intentionality based on Big Data.

This is not without precedence as the architecture of documentality can be associated with Friedrich Nietzsche's concept of *grand style*. He associated architecture with "the power which no longer needs any proof, which spurns pleasing, which does not answer lightly, […] which reposes within itself, fatalistically, a law among laws — that speaks of itself as a grand style"[3]. Architecture is a "kind of eloquence of power in forms". Nietzsche's example was Palazzo Pitti in Florence. In this building the architectural signs and stylistic elements are simplified to the point of caricature. In the excess of simplification and enlargement, they lose their meaning. They are only big and aim solely at *effect*.

Elsewhere, Nietzsche also speaks of the uncanny sublime, which he equates with the aesthetic category of the sublime. In doing so, he refers to the aesthetic of idealism, which contrasts the principle of beauty with the principle of the sublime. While beauty relies on order and clarity of meaning, the sublime, on the other hand, is an aesthetic event that does not explain how it came about. It achieves its strongest effect by leaving the sources of its origin in the dark. Hence, digital documentality ties in precisely with the concept of the sublime and transfers it into the digital age by shifting the cultural dominants.

New Monumentality

Today, artificial intelligence is the source for the great changes in architecture, which

なかの法に応答する力－つまり自身を偉大な様式として語るもの」と捉えました(注3)。建築は「フォルムにおける力の雄弁さのようなもの」です。ニーチェは、フィレンツェの「ピッティ宮殿」を例に挙げます。この建物においては、建築的記号や様式的要素は、カリカチュアにまで単純化されました。過剰な単純化と拡大によって記号やフォルムの要素は意味を失い、単に大きく、効果だけを追求しているのです。

他の議論のなかでニーチェは不気味さを持つ崇高性についても言及し、これを美学的な意味における崇高性と同等であるとし、そこではまた美しさの原則と崇高の原則を対比させた理想主義の美学に依拠しました。美しさは秩序と意味の明晰さに依存します。他方、崇高性はそれがどのように生じるかを説明しない美学的な事象です。その起源を不明にしておくことで、崇高性は最大限の効果を発揮します。したがって、ドキュメンタリティは崇高という概念と結びついており、幾多のシフトを重ねて、崇高性をデジタル時代へと移行させるのです。

新しいモニュメンタリティ

人工知能は今日、建築が大きく変化する源となっています。つまり、変化の推進力は建築分野の外から来ているということです。4度目のコペルニクス的転回の過程で、人工知能、ビッグデータ、データに基づくデザインによって、過去600年にわたり建築を定義してきた人文科学的な礎が変わりつつあります。建築における人文科学は、建築デザインを図面や模型で記録することを義務とする建築に結びついています。最初にこれを要求したのは、レオン・バッティ

means that the impulses for change come from outside architecture. In the course of the fourth Copernican revolution, artificial intelligence, big data and data-based design are changing the humanistic foundations of architecture, as they have defined architecture for the past 600 years. Humanism in architecture is linked to the commitment of architecture to the documentation of designs in drawings and models. Leon Battista Alberti (1404-72) was the first to demand this. Architecture became a matter of the drawing desk. This changed architecture fundamentally. When architecture was previously a matter for the building site, reference to other architects and other architecture was only possible to a limited extent. Drawing, on the other hand, enabled architects to make reference to other architectures and other times in an experimental form.

Documentation on paper made it possible to quote and collage styles, forms, and details of other architects on a trial basis. Eventually, this led architecture to become an intellectual and artistic practice. This turned architecture into a cultural technique equivalent to the arts, such as painting and sculpture and subsequently upgraded the role of the architect. From then on, architecture was reliant on the intentionality of the individual architect.

Watanabe takes up precisely this thinking and goes far beyond the factuality and supposed lack of alternatives of digital documentality. He is not at all satisfied with an architecture of pure effects and proposes an interesting alternative in this exhibition. He does not want to leave open the gap in the monumentality that big data and data based design have struck. On the contrary, in closing the gap he sees an opportunity for

スタ・アルベルティ（1404-72）でした。それ以前には建設現場での決定が建築そのものであり、他の建築家や建築への参照の可能性は限定的でしたが、図面の誕生によってそれが大きく可能となり、建築家が実験的な形で他の建築や時代を参照するようになりました。

　紙への記録によって、他の建築家や様式を試しに引用し、コラージュして、新たな関連性を作り出すことが可能になります。可視的な記号、装飾、様式フォルムを通じて、建築は自己の物質的存在を超越し、知的で芸術的な活動となってゆきました。そうして初めて、文化的技術としての建築が絵画や彫刻などの芸術と並ぶものになり、それ以来、建築は個々の建築家の志向性に強く依存してきたのです。

　渡邊さんはこの見方に立って、しかもデジタルのドキュメンタリティの事実性と、そこに想定される代案欠如性を遥かに超えていきます。彼は、純粋に効果を狙った建築に満足することなく、この展覧会では興味深い代案を見せています。そして、ビッグデータに基づくデザインがもたらした、モニュメンタリティの欠落をそのままにせず、逆にその欠落を埋めることにこそ、真に新しい建築を生み出すチャンスがあると考えています。彼は次のように書いています。「モニュメンタリティの空白を作るということは技術の空白を意図的に生み出すということです」、「モニュメンタリティの再生は新たにやってくる技術の価値観によってもたらされることになります」。

　渡邊さんは正当にも、モニュメンタリティの空白は、その空白を作った技術では埋められないことを指摘しています。つま

a truly new monumentality. He writes: "Creating a void of monumentality means intentionally creating a void of technology". And then he continues, "the renewal of monumentality emerges from the values of new technologies".

Watanabe rightly points out that the gap in monumentality cannot be closed by the technologies that have opened it. This task can only be entrusted to other technologies. The gap in monumentality is an opportunity for other more sophisticated technologies to bring architecture back to its basic function as a social object. Watanabe also provides historical examples for this. The gap that modern mass production has opened up in monumentality has not been closed by the very same serial technology that caused the problem, but precisely by the use of technologies from other areas, such as shipbuilding and aircraft construction, in other words, the technologies that enabled individual production in architecture, but at a higher and more sophisticated technological level than the old technologies that they replaced, such as masonry or timber construction. This is the kind of new monumentality that Crossover-Architecture is striving for.

Berlin, 8. April 2020

り、この役割は他の技術に任せるしかあり
ません。モニュメンタリティの空白を、よ
り洗練され攻撃性の低い他の技術によって
埋めるのは、社会的物体としての従来の機
能を建築に取り戻すためのチャンスです。
また、渡邊さんもそのような歴史的な例を
紹介しています。大量生産がもたらしたモ
ニュメンタリティの空白は、シリアル技術
によってではなく、造船や航空機製造など
他分野の技術、つまり建築の個別生産を再
び可能にするような技術によって埋められ
る、と彼は述べます。それらはかつて石造
や木造に取って代わった当の技術であり、
古典的技術よりも洗練された新たな技術レ
ベルでこれを使用することによって、モ
ニュメンタリティの空白が埋められるとい
うことです。「クロスオーバー・アーキテ
クチュア」という考えが示すのは、このよ
うな種類の新しいモニュメンタリティなの
です。

2020 年 4 月 8 日、ベルリン

■注釈
注 1 フレドリック・ジェイムソン "Postmodernism or,
The Cultural Logic of Late Capitalism" 第 3 章
〔https://www.marxists.org/reference/subject/
philosophy/works/us/jameson.htm〕
注 2 マウリツィオ・フェラーリス "Documentalità.
Perché è necessario lasciar tracce"（Roma-Bari、
Laterza、2009 年）
注 3 フリードリヒ・ニーチェ『偶像の黄昏』（1888 年）
の断章「反時代的人間の渉猟」アフォリズム
No.11（参考邦訳：河出文庫、村井則夫訳、
2019 年）。拙稿の論文 "»But Turin!«,
Nietzsche's Discovery of the City" 〔https://
www.architekturtheorie.tu-berlin.de/menue/
team/prof_dr_ing_ habil_joerg_h_gleiter/
parameter/de/〕も参照。

■ NOTES
1. Fredric Jameson, Postmodernism or, The Cultural Logic of
Late Capitalism, chpt. III, https://www.marxists.org/
reference/subject/philosophy/works/us/jameson.htm
(March 30, 2020)
2. Maurizio Ferraris, Documentalità. Perché è necessario
lasciar tracce, Roma-Bari: Laterza 2009.
3. Friedrich Nietzsche, Twilight of the Idols, "Skirmishes of an
Untimely Man", Aph. 11., see also Jörg H. Gleiter, »But
Turin!«, Nietzsche's Discovery of the City, https://www.
architekturtheorie.tu-berlin.de/menue/team/prof_dr_ing_
habil_joerg_h_gleiter/parameter/de/

Summary

人のための床、あるいは建築のための床
A floor for a person or building

伏見 唯
Yui FUSHIMI

　ひとえに建築に接するといっても、なかなか具体的な光景を思い描けないのではないか。人間に比べて大きすぎるから、焦点が定まらないのだ。しかし、床に接する姿ならば、すぐに想像できると思う。飛べない人間は、日々絶え間なく足元の床や地面と接している。アスファルトの道路か、木のフローリングか、絨毯か。それらは直接、あるいは靴や衣服を介して人体と触れるため、その材質の如何によって居心地が決まる。建築を構成する数多くの要素のなかでも、床はとりわけ人間の個体に寄り添った

It may be difficult to envisage concretely how people become exposed to architecture. Architecture is too big for our bodies to comprehend. But we easily and immediately imagine how we touch a floor. Since human beings cannot fly, we constantly make contact with floors and the ground with our feet every day. Our bodies touch asphalt roads, wooden flooring, or carpets directly or through shoes or clothing. The material determines the level of comfort we feel when touching a floor. Among the many elements that comprise architecture, flooring is perhaps the element most closely

部位の１つだろう。

人が居る場所に置かれていた畳

　日本の畳（注1）もまた、人間の身体と関わりの深い床材だ。「起きて半畳、寝て１畳」と言われ、１人の人間が占める面積が、例えば３尺×６尺（約910×1,820mm）ほどの畳１枚分や半分であることを示している。これは諺だが、実際に「六畳」「四畳半」などと部屋に敷き詰められた畳の枚数を示せば、自分の身の丈と照らし合わせておおよそその部屋の広さが感覚的に分かるから、「畳（帖）」は人体を通して部屋の大きさを表す尺度の単位でもある。

　その畳は、元々は床に敷き詰められることはなく、座布団のように人の居る場所だけに置かれた舗設（しつらい）だったことが分かっている。舗設は、日本古代の寝殿造の貴族住宅において、儀式などの際に場所を設えるための調度で、御簾、几帳、屏風などとともに置畳があった。寝殿造は、大きな寺院や宮殿を作るための建築技術を転用して築かれ、その内部は柱ばかりが林立したまさに大きな伽藍堂のような空間だったため、そうした舗設を使って居住用の小さな空間を作る必要があったと言われている（注2）。

　また、この頃の畳は後の規格化された畳ほど大きさは統一されていない。当時は序列が重要視される貴族社会であったため、座る人の身分が高いほど大きくて厚い畳が用いられ、時には重ねて用いられることもあったのだ。さらに身分にあわせて畳の縁の色や文様などを変えていたという（注3）。

　他人の視線を遮るためのちょっとした仕切りがほしい。板敷きの硬い床に座ったの

attuned to the human body.

Tatami mats in spaces that a person occupies

The Japanese tatami mat[1] is a flooring material deeply related to the human body. There is a Japanese expression that says, "Half a mat in the morning, and a mat at night". It means that the space of someone who is sitting or lying down is equivalent to half a tatami or a tatami with the dimensions of 3 x 6 shaku (approx. 910 x 1,820 mm). By showing or describing the number of tatami mats (for example, six tatami mats or 4.5 tatami mats) laid out in a room, you can imagine the approximate size of a room by comparing it with your own body. Tatami mats are a unit of measurement for a room size through the human body.

Originally, tatami was not laid on an entire floor. People considered it to be *shitsurai*, a smaller piece of furniture placed only where people sat, like a floor cushion. *Shitsurai* sprang from the furnishings used in the ancient Shinden-zukuri style (the architecture representative of a nobleman's residence during the Heian period [794-1185]) during ceremonies. It includes the tatami mat, bamboo blinds, curtained screens, and folding screens. Buildings in the Shinden-zukuri style adopted the architectural techniques used for making large temples and palaces. Because the interior was just like the hall of a large temple with only columns, people believed that they should divide a small residential space using these furnishings[2].

Significantly, the size of a tatami at that time was not as uniform it later became when standardized. In the aristocratic society of the period, the higher the rank of the person who sat on a tatami mat, the

では身体が痛い。使う人の身分にふさわしい場を演出したい。そうした人の想いを叶えるべく畳や屏風などの舗設で小回りを利かせ、大きな建築と小さな人間を調停していたのである。

畳を起点とした建築のつくり方に

その後、畳は部屋全体に敷き詰められていくようになる。敷き詰められると、1つひとつの畳の大きさや厚みを変えることは難しいが、畳がそこに座る人の立場を示す風習は一部残った。例えば茶室では、床の間の前に敷く「貴人畳」、客が座るところに敷く「客畳」、茶事の点前を行う場所に敷く「点前畳」などと同形の畳を場所によって呼び分けている。座す人に合わせて畳を変えるというよりは、畳に合わせて座すに近いと言ってもよいかもしれない。

また畳が敷き詰められた結果、近世の江戸時代には、規格化された畳を敷く枚数で部屋の大きさを決める畳割が広まる。例えば畳の長辺に襖2枚、天井の桟5本などと連鎖し、さらに建築の骨格である柱スパンも畳の枚数と関連して決まるために標準寸法が生まれ、畳を基準としながら建築の多くの部分が並行して規格化していった。こうした規格や標準寸法は広まりやすい。個別の事情を溶解させるほどの普及力で、支配階級から被支配階級の建築まで共通の技術でつくりえる生産力を発揮するにいたる（注4）。

こうして畳は人間の個体の事情に即したものから、建築の生産システムに組み込まれ社会の総体の基盤の1つになっていった。それでもなお畳が人体に端を発した尺度の延長にあることによって、人間が建築

larger and thicker it was, and it was sometimes used in layers. Furthermore, the colors and patterns of the edges of a tatami changed to suit their social status[3].

"We need a little screen to block other people's eyes". "I don't want to hurt my body by sitting directly on a hard wooden floor". "We want to create a space suitable for the position of a person who uses it". To meet such requests, small things, such as tatami mat and folding screens, make people fit into a larger space.

Building construction based on tatami mats

Over time, tatami mats began to cover the entire room. It was difficult to change the size and thickness of each tatami mat once they began covering rooms. However, the custom of expressing a person's status through a tatami mat remains. For example, in a tearoom, tatami mats have different names depending on where they are laid. A tatami in front of a *tokonoma* alcove, a seat of honor, is called *Kinin-datami* (a tatami for a noble person). A tatami for where guests sit is called *Kyaku-datami* (a tatami for a guest). A tatami for where a host makes tea is called *Temae-datami* (a tatami for making tea). A person sits on the mat that is suitable for their position, rather than changing the mat to accord with the user's status.

During the Edo period (1603-1867), the size of tatami mats became unified once tatamis began covering entire rooms. Tatamiwari, which determines the size of a room by the number of tatami mats, became a popular method of planning. For example, the length of the long side of a tatami mat is equivalent to the length of two fusuma doors (Japanese sliding doors) and five crosspieces on a ceiling. One determines

に合わせなければいけなくなったというよりは、むしろ建築が身体化されたと思わせるところに、畳の数奇な道程が凝縮されている。

　敷き込むと畳の位置が固定されることから、畳職人のあいだでは畳の短辺から入ってくる光を「縦明かり」、長辺からの光を「横明かり」と呼ぶ。同じ畳でも、仄暗いなかでの光の受け方で人が感じる表情が変わってくることを捉えたものだ。建築生産の起点に据えられながらも、依然として畳は、大きな建築の論理を小さな人間が見て取れる様相に翻訳しつづけていた。

人と接する身近なものの複合としての建築

　一方現代では、すでに畳割の生産体系はほぼなくなっているため、和室に畳が敷かれていたからといって、そこから建築の全体性を感じることはないだろう。畳を単なる和室の床材として、伝統的な日本のアイコンと見なすのではないのならば、何人かの近代の建築家がすでに試みてきたように、いっそ古代のあり方に戻って、座布団のような個別の人間に即した柔軟な使い方に戻してみるほうが運用の展開に幅は広がりそうだ。

　ただし、具体的な畳の使い方を検討するばかりではなく、本展で注目している「分野をまたぐ複合体」としての建築のことを考えるならば、寝殿造の舗設がまさに様々な人間の所作に対応した事物の複合であったし、その複合の一部が近世までの時の流れのなかで建築全体の生産システムに組み込まれ、社会の隅々まで敷衍していった経歴が見過ごせない。

　やはり建築は人体と比べて大きすぎるの

the span of columns, the framework of architecture, in relation to the number of tatami mats and standard dimensions created. Many building parts were standardized according to the size of tatami mats. These standards and dimensions spread quickly. Standardization led to increased productivity through common technologies, which extremely spread from the buildings of the ruling classes to those under rule[4].

In this way, the tatami mat changed from one adapted to human bodies to something that the production system of architecture incorporated and became a foundation of society. Nevertheless, because a tatami is an extension of the scale that originated from the human body, the notion that architecture itself has become embodied rather than that human bodies have to conform to architecture encapsulates tatami's odd journey.

The position of tatami is fixed after it is laid down. Tatami craftsmen call the light coming in from the short side of a tatami "vertical light" and the light from the long side "sidelight". These names show how people feel changes depending on how they receive light in the dark. While the tatami mat became the starting point of architecture production, it continued to be the element that translated large architecture logically into ways people could visualize.

Architecture as a composite of familiar objects in contact with people

In contrast, today, the production system of *tatamiwari* has almost disappeared. Thus, even if tatami appeared in a Japanese-style room, it will not make you feel the totality of architecture. Tatami is a traditional Japanese icon and not merely flooring material for a

だ。それを建ち上げる難解な技術や表現と向き合っているなかで、すぐに人間が置き去りにされうる。人と接する身近なものの複合として建築を顧みるならば、建築に接する姿も迷わず具体的に思い描けるようになるのではないか。

床一面に敷き詰められた畳
The room covered by tatami mats

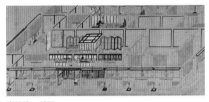

寝殿造の舗設
『類聚雑要抄』(部分)東京国立博物館イメージアーカイブ
Shitsurai in the ancient Shinden-zukuri style
(via TNM Image Archives)

Japanese-style room. For various ways of using tatami, it would be better to go back to the ancient style, as some modern architects have done, and return it to the more flexible way that individuals once used, such as floor cushion.

However, if we not only consider the actual usage of tatami but also think of architecture as a "multidisciplinary complex" that attracts attention in this exhibition, we can see that the furnishings in the Shinden-zukuri style are a composite of things that correspond to various human behaviors. Notably, a part of the complex was incorporated into the production system of the whole building over time until modern times, and developed in every corner of society.

After all, architecture is too big for the human body to grasp. Human beings are quickly left behind when they confront the esoteric techniques and expressions within architecture. If we can regard architecture to be a complex of familiar things that are in contact with people, I think we will envision how architecture interacts with people without hesitation.

■注釈
注1 日本の伝統的な床材。藁などを原料とした板状の「畳床」に、藺草で織った敷物の「畳表」を取り付けたもの。1枚あたりの伝統的な規格サイズには、京間 3.15 尺 × 6.3 尺（約 955 × 1910mm）、中京間 3 尺 × 6 尺 ×（約 910 × 1,820mm）、田舎間 2.9 尺 × 5.8 尺（約 880 × 1,760mm）などがある。
注2 小泉和子、玉井哲雄、黒田日出男編『絵巻物の建築を読む』東京大学出版会、1996 年。
注3 山田幸一監修、佐藤理著『物語ものの建築史 畳のはなし』鹿島出版会、1985 年。
注4 渡辺保忠「工業化への道《NO1》工業化への道のなかで職人はどう変化して来たか」(『建築史学』Vol.35 に再録)。

■ NOTES
1. Traditional Japanese flooring material. Tatami is made by attaching *Tatami omote*, a mat woven with rush, to *Tatami doko*, a plate-like compressed straw. The traditional standard sizes for a piece include 3.15 x 6.3 shaku (approx. 955 x 1,910 mm) for *Kyoma*, 3 x 6 shaku (approx. 910 x 1,820 mm) for *Chukyoma*, and 2.9 x 5.8 shaku (approx. 880 x 1,760 mm) for *Inakama*.
2. Kazuko KOIZUMI, Tetsuo TAMAI, Hideo KURODA, 1996. *Emakimono no kenchiku wo yomu*. Tokyo: University of Tokyo Press.
3. Kouichi YAMADA, Osamu SATO, 1985. *Monogatari monono kenchikushi tatami no hanashi*. Tokyo: Kashima Publishing.
4. Yasutada WATANABE. "Kogyoka eno michi <<NO1>> Kogyoka eno michi no naka de shokunin ha dou henka shite kitaka". Kenchiku Shigaku 35.

3

Exhibitions

3 Synesthesia Scenery

ユニティ・アーキテクチュア／実践編
ワイマール展
Unity Architecture / Practice Edition
Exhibition in Weimar

Synesthesia Scenery

Japanese Arts and Crafts at
the Dawn of the Modern Age
@Bauhaus-Universität Weimar
Conceived and curated by
Taishi WATANABE

ワイマール展カタログ表紙
Catalog Cover for the Exhibition in Weimar

　ワイマールでの「Synesthesia Scenery」展の扉絵には、展示物のなかから縄とペーパーナイフ、そしてメダルを採用しています。手のなかにある物体を何に使えるかと考えるとき、常に形態は機能から解放された状態にあるはずです。初期設定からそのような状態にある物をオブジェクトと呼び、そのオブジェクト同士の間に働く人間の意識を空間と呼ぶならば、建築もまた機能的な部品の集合ではない別のオブジェクトの集合体と見ることができるでしょう。

　ワイマールでは、バウハウス創立当初の教室であった温室ガラス屋根を持つ会場の内側にプリントされた展示物の写真を並べることで、この教室そのものを「Synesthesia Scenery」の実態として捉えることができるように意図しています。

On the cover art of the catalogue of the "Synesthesia Scenery" exhibition in Weimar, we selected the rope, the paper knife, and the medal from the exhibits. When we think the usage of an item in our hands, the form must be always released from the function. If the items in such a status from the beginning are called "objects" and the human consciousness between the "objects" is called "space", we can also consider architecture as a collection of other "objects" that are not functional parts.

In Weimar, by arranging the printed photos of the exhibits in the site that was a classroom in the infancy of Bauhaus and has a greenhouse glass roof, we intend you to understand this classroom itself as the substance of "Synesthesia Scenery".

「None-scale materiality」の実践

Practice of "no-scale material"

渡邊大志
Taishi WATANABE

ワイマールでの展覧会は、異なる芸術・デザイン・材料が互いに鑑賞者の異なる五感に働きかけることで作り出す空間風景を「Synesthesia Scenery（共感覚空間）」と呼び、その視点から日本の近現代建築のいくつかを紹介するものです。

その目的は、建築に専門化された現代のデザインと技術の体系を疑い、元々あらゆる造形物に備わっている Synesthesia（共感覚）という性質をデザインによって活性化することで、改めて建築を作り上げていくことにあります。

This exhibition introduces forms of modern and contemporary Japanese architecture from "synesthesia scenery" perspective, which is a spatial landscape that different arts, designs, and materials that engage the viewers' five senses create by interacting with one another.

The purpose of this project is to reinvigorate the nature of synesthesia, which is inherent in all forms through design, by questioning the contemporary system of design and technology specialized in architecture.

ご存知のように、ワイマール・バウハウスは世界で最初の近代建築学校です。そのオリジナルカリキュラムでは、分野の枠に納まらないデザインの実験が多く行われていました。

　今日では一般的にバウハウスのデザインは白い四角いキューブや直線によるコンポジションを想起させます。しかし、それらはバウハウスから発信された唯一のデザインの可能性ではありません。初代校長となったワルター・グロピウスだけでなく、設立当初のバウハウスにはヨハネス・イッテン、オスカー・シュレンマー、モホイ・ナギ、パウル・クレー、ワンリー・カンディンスキーといった錚々たるメンバーが日々その分野と材料の区別のない実験的なデザインを試みていました。彼らがアンリ・ヴァンデ・ベルデの設計による旧工芸学校をモダニズムの拠点として再利用したことにも、分野を持たない前衛的なデザインの理念を垣間見ることができます。

　色彩論、造形論、身体芸術論といった問いの立て方とそのネーミングは、絵画、彫刻、演劇、音楽、建築などの最終的な表現形式による認識方法を無効にしてしまうとても戦略的な思考体系でした。

　しかしながら、モダニズム自体が100年単位の歴史を持つに至るプロセスのなかで、生産性と技術伝承の合理性による近代化は建築の専門分化を加速度的に進めました。そのオリジンにおいて本来目指されていた分野に縛られず互いに干渉し合うデザインの希求は、むしろ非合理なものとされています。

　20世紀末のコンピュータの登場により、生産者と消費者を直に接続する情報化は、

Bauhaus Weimar was the first modern architecture school in the world. In the original curriculum, numerous design experiments did not fit within the field's boundaries. Today, the Bauhaus design generally reminds us of the images of white, square cubes and linear compositions. But they are not the only design possibilities originating from the Bauhaus. In addition to Walter Gropius, the first principal of the school, the original Bauhaus comprised a team of eminent designers and artists, including Johannes Itten, Oscar Schremmer, Moholy-Nagy, Paul Klee, and Vasily Kandinsky, who were attempting to create experimental designs without distinguishing between fields and materials. Reusing the old craft school that Henry van de Velde had designed as a basis for modernism gives us a glimpse into the philosophy of avant-garde design with no field.

The manner in which questions were raised and names were given, such as color theory, modeling theory, and physical art, was an extremely strategic thinking structure that nullified the recognition method based on the final form of expression, such as painting, sculpture, drama, music, and architecture.

However, as modernism developed over 100-year history, modernization based on the productivity and rationality of technology transfer accelerated the specialization of architecture. Seeking designs that interfere with each other without the original field binding them becomes rather irrational.

With the advent of computers at the end of the 20th century, the computerization

確かに近代化の成果である「機械化による産業化」をそれ以前の個人単位での取引の次元に引き戻したと言えます。しかしその一方では、情報化はグローバル経済をより一層加速させた生産的合理性と投資の回収までの速さの合理性に価値を置く社会全体が、「個別解であることによる普遍解」による未来を共有することは課題とされたままです。

近代的な産業化の術として大量生産を目的とした標準化と規格化以外の合理的方法を私たちが持たないことが、昨今世界中で求められるイノベーション・ダイバーシティ・サステナビリティを達成するために旧態依然とした大量生産の理論と方法を用い続ける、という根本的な矛盾の原因であると考えます。

そのとき、未来のデザインには何ができるでしょうか。この問題を解くためには、現在のグローバルな流通商品としての芸術・デザインの起源を再検討し、そこに伏在した別の道を再発見する必要があります。

その1つの実践として、ここでは芸術・デザインであるオブジェクトがその材質によって互いの Synesthesia を強める場合について考えてみたいと思います。端末であるそれぞれのオブジェクトがブロックチェーンのように連動して全体の空間領域を作り出している状態を想像してみてください。

1つの空間に閉じた建物の場合は、機能主義に基づく見方によってもそれは1つの閉じられた機能体に見えるため、その建物の内部空間が Synesthesia によって生

that directly connected producers and consumers could bring the "industrialization through mechanization" that resulted from modernization back to the individual-level transactions that preceded it. On the other hand, sharing the future of the "universal solution as an individual solution" remains a problem for society as a whole, which values the productive rationality that further accelerated the global economy and the rationality of the speed of investment recovery.

I believe that the absence of rational methods other than standardization and standardization for the purpose of mass production as a modern method of industrialization have caused a fundamental contradiction. This is the continued use of the old-fashioned theories and methods of mass production to achieve the innovation, diversity, and sustainability required worldwide today.

What can we do with future designs? To solve this problem, one needs to reexamine the origin of art and design, which are globally distributed products today and rediscover another way that lies there. As an example of this practice, I would like to consider the case where objects that are art and design reinforce each other's "synesthesia" through their materials. Imagine that each object is a terminal that works together with other terminals like a blockchain to create the entire space.

In the case of a building that is enclosed as a single space, it may be difficult to recognize that the interior space of the building is caused by

じたものと認識することは難しいかもしれません。しかし、もし建築を構成する芸術・デザインのオブジェクトが点でバラバラに配されて 1 つの内部空間として閉じていなかったとしたら、それら複数のオブジェクトに点線で囲まれた領域を 1 つの空間として認識することはとても簡単なことでしょう。しかもそれと同時に、その空間領域が屋外か室内かは本質的な空間原理の違いに何ら関係がないことも分かるはずです。

　例えば、今もワイマールに残るグロピウスが設計監修した「7 人の兵士のための慰霊碑」や、イッテンがデザインした「廃墟の教室」には既にそのような性質が備わっています。

　ここでは、そのような性質を持ったオブジェクトを「None-scale materiality」と呼びたいと思います。それはつまり、全体のブロックチェーンによって作用される端末であると同時に、その全体を主体的に作動させて管理するオブジェクトには、従来の建築におけるスケールという概念が初めから存在しないという性質を意味しています。

　そして本展覧会では、全体のブロックチェーンと言える「Synesthesia Scenery」の姿を象る「None-scale materiality」とみなすことができるオブジェクトを次のように定義したいと思います。

1. 個別の差異を持った様相を呈するが、同一の手順によって生産・製作される
2. ハンドメイドに代表される、不確定

synesthesia because it appears to be a single, enclosed functional body, even from a functionalist perspective. However, if the art and design objects that compose architecture were separated and not enclosed as a single interior space, it would be extremely easy to see the area enclosed by the dotted lines between the objects as a single space. Concurrently, it should be understood that whether the space is outdoors or indoors has nothing to do with the essential difference in spatial principle. For example, the "Cenotaph for the Seven Soldiers", which was designed by Gropius and which remains in Weimar, and "Abandoned Classroom", designed by Itten, have such a spatial characteristic.

　I would like to define an object of this nature as a "no-scale material". This means that objects that operate and manage the entire blockchain on their own, as well as being terminals that are operated by the entire blockchain, do not have the traditional architectural concept of scale at all.

　In this exhibition, I would like to define an object that can be regarded as a no-scale material in the image of synesthesia scenery that can constitute the whole blockchain, as follows:

1. The same process produces it, but with the appearance of individual differences.
2. It includes a factor that renders the shape indeterminate, such as being handmade, in the design.
3. It is a piece of art or design in its own right, but without enclosing its

造形因子がそのデザインに含まれる

3. それ自体が独立した芸術・デザインであるが、その内に唯一の機能を閉じない

その上で本展では、日本最古の現存する木造建築物である法隆寺五重塔（6世紀）に用いられた鍛造釘を復元し、これを「None-scale materiality」の具体的なマイルストーンとしました。建設当時、高さ35.1mあるこの塔は日本で一番高い塔であったことでしょう。地震が多い日本において、これだけの高さを持つ塔を木造で建設するのは困難です。そのため木組みの裏には鍛造によって作られた隠し釘が用いられていることが分かっています。それら鍛造釘は全く同じ製法と手順で職人によって作られたものですが、それぞれが微妙に異なる形状をしています。そして展示の図版で示すように、それら鍛造釘は木造の架構のなかにピッチを刻むようにして穿たれています。その木組みも自然の木によるものですから、当然同じ目や節を持った材料は存在しません。このような構築物の在り方を建築単位で現れた「Synesthesia Scenery」と考え、鍛造釘の1本1本や複数の木材による肘木などの木組みを「None-scale materiality」と見ることから始めたいと思います。

その他の展示物はこの構図をさらに単体の建築から解放することを意図しています。それらは全て日本の近現代建築のいくつかから切り取られた断片です。特に本来の建築の全体像をご存じない鑑賞者のみなさんには、自然とそれらはそれぞれが独立した「None-scale materiality」というオ

sole function within it.

In this exhibition, we restored the forged nails used in the five-story pagoda of the Horyuji Temple built in the sixth century (which is Japan's oldest existing wooden building) and made them a concrete milestone for the term "no-scale material" defined above. At the time, this 35.1-meter tall tower must have been the tallest tower in Japan. Because numerous earthquakes occur in Japan, building such a high wooden tower is difficult. Therefore, it is known that hidden forged nails were used inside the wooden frame. Craftsmen made these forged nails using exactly the same processes and procedures, but they are not identically shaped. As shown in the illustration on display, these forged nails were carved into a wooden frame at specific intervals. Naturally, no wooden material has the same grain pattern because the wooden framework is made of natural wood. I would like to start thinking of this type of structure as a synesthesia scenery that appears in building units, and looking at the wooden frame of each forged nail or wood joinery made of multiple pieces of wood as a no-scale material.

The other exhibits are intended to further liberate the structure from stand-alone architecture. They are all fragments of forms of modern Japanese architecture. In particular, to those who do not have a complete overview of the original architecture, they will naturally look like separate objects called no-scale materials. In this manner, the exhibit becomes an object called a no-scale material, which reinforces the

ブジェクトに見えてしまうでしょう。そのようにして展示物が「None-scale materiality」というオブジェクトになることで、それぞれのオブジェクトが本来持っているSynesthesia が強められます。そしてその結果、それらの一部や全てが互いに連動して複数の異なる「Synesthesia Scenery」を形成する、ということを試みました。

　要するに、ここで紹介する展示物としてのオブジェクトは、それ自身の内に「Synesthesia Scenery」を持つと同時に、それらが独立した「None-scale materiality」であることで互いに異なる複数の「Synesthesia Scenery」を生み出す、という3重の仕掛けがなされています。それが展示物と展示空間との関係そのものとして現れています。

　加えて、本展覧会をバウハウス設立最初期の教室が復元された空間で行うことには、さらなる Synesthesia の連鎖を生むことが意図されています。

　すなわち、本展では会場である最初のバウハウス教室と共に、同じ中庭に面した有名な階段室を持つアンリ・ヴァンデ・ベルデ設計の校舎をも「None-scale materiality」とみなすことが意図されています。そして教室上部の温室ガラス越しに、それらと展示物とのより大きく複層的な「Synesthesia Scenery」が生まれることを意識しました。

　つまり、展覧会による Synesthesia の空間は会場のなかにあるだけでなく、展示物が会場の内外から見えることでその外の中庭自体を展覧会空間と化します。さらには、ほぼ人間の頭の高さまである石張りの壁部分より上部全面の温室ガラスを透過して展示物を見せることで、バウハウスのオ

underlying synesthesia of each object. Consequently, some or all of them try to cooperate to form multiple synesthesia sceneries.

In short, the objects introduced here as exhibits perform triple trick of incorporating synesthesia scenery within themselves and creating multiple synesthesia sceneries by being independent no-scale materials. That constitutes the relationship between the exhibits and the exhibition space itself. In addition, holding the exhibition in the restored space of the Bauhaus's original classroom is intended to create a further chain of synesthesia.

I intended this exhibition to consider Henry van de Velde's school building, which has a famous staircase facing the same courtyard as the first Bauhaus classroom, as a no-scale material. The exhibits are placed so that a larger, more multi-layered synesthesia scenery of the building and the exhibits could be created through the greenhouse glass at the top of the classroom.

In other words, the exhibition space of synesthesia is not only inside the exhibition hall but also the inner courtyard itself becomes an exhibition space because the exhibits can be seen from inside and outside the hall. The exhibition is also intended to temporarily redesign the elevation of Bauhaus's original classroom by showing the exhibits through the glass of the greenhouse above the stone-lined walls almost to the height of the viewers' heads. Therefore, I would like the visitors to see the exhibition again from outside through the courtyard along with the

リジナル教室の立面を仮設的に再デザインしてしまうことも意図しました。

　ですので、みなさんにはアンリ・ヴァンデ・ベルデの校舎とともに是非外からも中庭越しに再度展示をご覧いただきたく思います。

　このような展覧会と展示を考える上で、私の母国である日本の近現代建築のいくつかから具体的な素材を選んだ理由は、世界でも特殊な日本の近現代建築の事情によるものです。

　江戸時代と呼ばれる近世まで日本は鎖国政策を採っていました。当然外国との交流が全く無かった訳ではありませんが、そのため日本の近代化は欧米諸国の技術と文化

school buildings of Henry van de Velde.

　I chose specific materials from some of the modern and contemporary architecture in Japan, my home country, when considering exhibitions because the modern and contemporary architecture in Japan is unique in the world.

　Until 1853, Japan had adopted a policy of seclusion from foreign countries. Naturally, it interacted little with foreign countries, but Japan's modernization was generated by importing technologies and cultures from Western countries after the end of the isolation. Architecture is included in the technologies. For Japanese architects, who imported the concept of modern

校舎の中庭にあるバウハウス・アトリエとガラス越しの展示物（コラージュ作製：渡邊大志研究室）
Bauhaus. Atelier, collage by Taishi WATANABE Lab.

の輸入によってもたらされました。日本人にとっての建築もその一つです。近代建築という概念が初めから輸入によってもたらされた日本の建築家にとっては、建築家という社会的ポジションや自分たちの建築デザインの対価の正統性の証明は今に至るまで大きな命題であり続けています。特に建築物の設計施工においては、江戸時代までの木工大工の棟梁を中心とした建設文化（建築文化ではない）は現代の日本の建築の重要な背景を担っています。それは日本の近現代建築や建築家にとっては時にアイデンティティの問題として重くのし掛かってきたのです。

　しかしながら、バウハウスの設立当初に見られた、今は決して主流とは言えない芸術・デザインの別の可能性を再発見しようとしたのと同じように、このような日本の特殊な近代の状況のなかにも均質化とは異なるグローバル・デザインの道があると私は思います。

　本展覧会で紹介する展示物はその製作過程において、建築以外の職人の手や技術が大きく働いて実現されたものです。つまり、建築を欧米から輸入せねばならなかった日本は、その代わりに建築以外の芸術・デザイン、技術、職人を集めて建築を作ることに長けていたと読み替えることができると考えました。このアイデアは、20世紀の成果である標準化・規格化・均質化が完了した世界では、その閉塞を打破するヒントとなるでしょう。

　そのようにしてできた建築という概念を改めて「Synesthesia Scenery」と呼んでみたいと思います。ここまで読んで下さっ

architecture from the beginning, the proof of the social position of architects and the legitimacy of the value of their architectural designs have been a major issue to this day. In the design and construction of buildings in particular, the construction culture, not architectural culture, centered on the Japanese master carpenters until the Edo period (1603-1868) and played a critical role in modern Japanese architecture. It has sometimes been a matter of identity for modern and contemporary Japanese architecture and architects.

However, in the same manner that when Bauhaus was founded, the school tried to rediscover other possibilities of art and design that are not currently mainstream, I think a path exists for global design that differs from homogenization in this special modern situation in Japan.

The exhibits introduced in this exhibition were made possible by the great efforts of craftsmen other than architects in the production process. In other words, Japan, which had to import the technology of architecture from Europe and the United States, excelled at creating architecture by combining arts, designs, techniques, and craftsmen, other than architects. This idea could be a clue to break through the blockage in a world where standardization and homogenization, the achievement of the 20th century, have been completed.

I would like to call this concept of architecture synesthesia scenery. Those readers who have read this far, or who have actually seen the venue, will see

た方、実際に会場をご覧いただいた方には、もはやその空間領域が1つに閉じた空間であるかどうかは問題とならないことがよくお分かりになるでしょう。その Synesthesia を発するオブジェクト「None-scale materiality」による実践の感覚を感じていただけたなら幸いです。

そしてどの国や地域、人種や宗教に属する方々もご自身が生まれ育った環境になぞらえながら、それぞれ異なる「Synesthesia Scenery」の姿をここに見て下さったとしたら、それはデザインや建築の未来にとって大変喜ばしいことだと思います。

that it no longer matters whether the space is closed. It would be great if you could feel the sense of practice with the no-scale material objects that provide synesthesia.

And if people from any country, region, race, or religion were here to see a different synesthesia scenery of their own, comparing it to the environment in which they were born and raised, that would be extremely gratifying for the future of design and architecture.

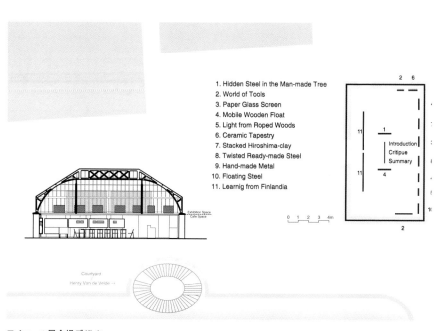

1. Hidden Steel in the Man-made Tree
2. World of Tools
3. Paper Glass Screen
4. Mobile Wooden Float
5. Light from Roped Woods
6. Ceramic Tapestry
7. Stacked Hiroshima-clay
8. Twisted Ready-made Steel
9. Hand-made Metal
10. Floating Steel
11. Learnig from Finlandia

Exhibition Space
Cafe Space

0 1 2 3 4m

Introduction
Critipue
Summary

Courtyard

Henry Van de Velde →

ワイマール展会場デザイン Exhibition-gallery Diagram

バウハウス大学ワイマール校／バウハウス・アトリエ Bauhaus.Atelier, Bauhaus-Universität Weimar

Critique

ワイマール展に関する考察

Reflections on the exhibition
Synesthesia Scenery in Weimar

ヴェレーナ・フォン・ベッケラス
建築家、ワイマール・バウハウス大学教授

Verena VON BECKERATH
Architect and professor at
Bauhaus-Universität Weimar

親愛なる渡邊さんへ

　ヘルシンキ・アアルト大学での１年間の研究プロジェクトの成果を、バウハウス大学ワイマール校でのSynesthesia Sceneryと題された展覧会で発信するというあなたの決定を嬉しく思います。ヘルシンキ、ベルリン、東京に加えて、ワイマールはあなたの展覧会にとって興味深い場所です。

　あなたのプロジェクトは、社会的、経済的、文化的条件を含む日本の伝統と近代化

Dear Watanabe-san,

　I was pleased about your decision to show the results of your one-year research project at Aalto University in Helsinki in an exhibition entitled *Synesthesia Scenery* at the Bauhaus-Universität Weimar. Besides Helsinki, Berlin and Tokyo, Weimar is an interesting place for your exhibition.

　Your research project is concerned with the traditions and modernisation of Japan, including its social, economic and cultural conditions, and is a direct result of these.

に関連しており、それこそがあなたのプロジェクトの直接的な成果です。また、それと同時に建築において一般化されている原則に疑問を投げかけています。この疑問は、特定の土地の伝統や物語の背景に対して真の意味をもたらします。あなたが提示する作品群は、アートとヒューマニズム、手仕事による材料と現代技術の調和に取り組んでいます。レプリカや工芸品、画像、コラージュといった連想的なコレクションは、拡張したり、新しく順序立てたりすることができ、ハンブルクの美術史家アビ・ヴァールブルク（1866-1929）による「ムネモシュネ・アトラス」を想起させます。アビ・ヴァールブルクは、1920年代に、様々な時代や文化的背景の相互影響に従ってイメージを認識し、配置する方法を発明しました。この作品が最後に記録されたバージョンは、2020年秋にベルリンの「世界文化の家」において「Aby Warburg：Bilderatlas Mnemosyne–Das Original」というタイトルで展示されました。一緒に展覧会について話をする機会を楽しみにしています。

　あなたがワイマールにこのプロジェクトの準備のために来たのは、2019年12月のある日のことでした。市と大学が歴史的なバウハウス100周年を祝っていた年が終わりに近づいていました。バウハウス博物館の新しい建物とコレクションはすでに春にオープンし、ワイマール新美術館は1900年頃の初期モダニズムの芸術作品を展示していました。デッサウとベルリンもバウハウス専用の美術館を計画中、あるいは、現在進行中です。これらのドイツ全土における展覧会、会議、出版物は、ヴァル

You also ask questions about universal principles in architecture, which only gain their true meaning against the backdrop of local traditions and narratives. Your work addresses the reconciliation of handcrafted materials and contemporary technologies, of art and humanism. The associative collection of replicas and artefacts, images and collages, which can be expanded or newly arranged, reminds me of the *Mnemosyne Atlas* by the Hamburg art historian Aby Warburg (1866-1929). Aby Warburg had invented a method in the 1920s to perceive and arrange images from different eras and cultural contexts according to their interaction. The last documented version of this work will be shown in the autumn at Haus der Kulturen der Welt, Berlin, with the title *Aby Warburg: Bilderatlas Mnemosyne – Das Original*. Perhaps we will have the opportunity to visit the exhibition together and talk about it.

　It was on a day in December 2019 that you came for a preparatory visit to Weimar. The year the city and university had been celebrating the 100th anniversary of the historic Bauhaus was drawing to a close. The new building and collection for the Bauhaus Museum Weimar had already opened in the spring and the Neues Museum Weimar was showing works of art of Early Modernism around 1900. Dessau and Berlin are also planning museums dedicated to the Bauhaus or are still in the process of converting them. Exhibitions, conferences and publications throughout Germany illuminate the school that was founded by Walter Gropius as Staatliches Bauhaus in Weimar, moved to Dessau in 1925 where Hannes Meyer was director, had to close under pressure from the National

ター・グロピウスによってワイマールにバ
ウハウスとして設立され、1925 年にハン
ネス・マイヤーを校長としてデッサウに移
動したこの学校が、国家社会主義政権から
の圧力の下で閉鎖しなければならず、
1933 年にミース・ファン・デル・ローエ
の下で解散するまで、制限された条件下で
最終的にベルリンに存在し続けたことを明
らかにしています。バウハウスの歴史は複
雑であり、実在した短い期間についての見
方は多様で、他のモダニズムとの相互関係
は部分的にしか考察されていません。その
冬の日に、私たちはあなたの展覧会とバウ
ハウス初期の時代の関連性について話し合
い、適切な展示場所を探りました。

2019/2020 年の冬学期に、私たちと学
部の何人かの学生は、現在博物館として訪
れることができるワイマールのいくつかの
歴史的建造物を調査しました。ニーチェの
アーカイブを除いてすべてが実際に居住さ
れていたそれらの家で、私たちはスケッチ
を描きながら住宅建築について学びたいと
思っていました。さらに私たちは写真家ア
ンドリュー・アルバーツを招きました。ご
存知のように、私たちはこのプロジェクト
の過程で、1930 年代と 1940 年代の東京
郊外の 2 軒の家を調査しました。これに
より、「Two Houses」(2019) という映画
を制作し、それらの建物を題材にして、建
築家について伝記と日本におけるモダニズ
ムやバウハウスの影響に対する有用性につ
いての物語をまとめた「Two Houses」と
いう本を出版しました。ベルヴェーデラー・
アレー58 番地に建つ「ホーヘ・パペルン邸」
は、1908 年にアンリ・ヴァン・デ・ヴェ

Socialist regime and finally continued to
exist in Berlin under restricted conditions
until its self-dissolution under Mies van der
Rohe in 1933. The history of the Bauhaus is
complex, the perspectives on the short
period of its existence are diverse, and its
interrelation with other strands of modernism
has only partially been explored. On that
winter's day, we talked about the possible
links between your exhibition and the early
Bauhaus years and looked for a suitable
location.

In the winter semester 2019/2020, we
and some students at our faculty studied
several historic buildings in Weimar, which
now can be visited as museums. In those
houses, all of which were inhabited except
for the Nietzsche archive, we hoped to learn
about residential architecture while drawing,
and we invited the photographer Andrew
Alberts to join us. As you know, we have
studied two houses from the 1930s and
1940s in the suburbs of Tokyo in the course
of a research project. This gave rise to the
Two Houses (2019) film and the *Two Houses
– Texts* publication that examine the
buildings, the biographies of their architects
and the narrative of their use against the
backdrop of modernism and the influence of
the Bauhaus on Japan. The Haus Hohe
Pappeln on Belvederer Allee 58 was
designed by Henry van de Velde (1863-
1957) in 1908 for his family, who lived there
until 1918. Henry van de Velde had not
studied architecture but trained as a fine
artist and later concentrated on interiors and
the detailed design of everyday objects,
using various materials such as porcelain,
glass, ceramics, textiles and metal.
Anonymous Japanese craftsmanship had a
considerable influence on his work. The

ホーへ・パペルン邸の書斎（左）と玄関ホールのディテール、撮影：アンドリュー・アルバーツ、2019 年
Study and detail of the vestibule at Haus Hohe Pappeln. Photography: Andrew Alberts, 2019

バウハウス大学ワイマール校メイン校舎 1 階の 102 号教室（左）と手前にあるスタジオ風景、撮影：ロバート・エーレルト、2017 年
Room 102 on the first floor of the main building at Bauhaus-Universität Weimar and view of the former studio. Photography: Robert Elert, 2017

ルデ（1863-1957）によって、1918年までそこに住んでいた家族のために設計されました。アンリ・ヴァン・デ・ヴェルデは建築を学んでいませんでしたが、優れた芸術家として訓練を受け、その後、磁器、ガラス、陶磁器、テキスタイル、金属などの様々な素材を使用して、インテリアと日常のオブジェクトの細部にこだわったデザインに集中しました。匿名の日本の職人技が彼の作品に大きな影響を与えました。ホーヘ・パペルン邸の書斎と前庭の写真の並置は、初期モダニズムからモダニズムへの移行における構造の抽象性と具体性の驚くべき同時性を示しており、ワイマールにおけるバウハウス初期の心髄と出現の前兆を示しています。

1886年に建てられた大公立美術工芸学校の校長と動物画家の元スタジオは、現在のキャンパスの中心にあるバウハウス大学ワイマール本館の南側にあります。それは、2つの現代スタジオの建物とベルヴェーデラー・アレー1番地に建つグリュンダーツァイトスタイルの別荘で構成されます。小さな建物は地元のトラバーチンで建てられており、四方に傾斜したガラスの屋根があります。バウハウス校のカフェテリアは、1919年から1925年までここにありました。スタジオは、1990年代後半まで保管スペースとして使用されていましたが、その後、学生が経営するカフェと小さな書店になりました。本館の中央の階段と上層階から見ることができます。本館は、新しく設立された美術工芸学校のために1911年にアンリ・ヴァン・デ・ヴェルデによって設計され、数年後にバウハウスが入居しま

juxtaposition of photographs of the study and the vestibule at the Haus Hohe Pappeln shows an astonishing simultaneity of structural abstraction and materiality in the transition from Early Modernism to Modernism and is a premonition of the emergence and focus of the early years of the Bauhaus in Weimar.

The former studio of an animal painter and director of the Großherzoglich-Sächsischen Kunstschule, which was built in 1886, is situated on the south side of the Bauhaus-Universität Weimar's main building in the centre of the current campus, comprising the Prellerhaus, two contemporary studio buildings and a villa in the Gründerzeit style at Belvederer Allee 1. The small building is constructed from local travertine and has sloping glass roofs on all sides. The cafeteria of the Staatliches Bauhaus was located here from 1919 to 1925. The studio was used as a storage space until the late 1990s and then turned into a café that is run by students and a small book shop. It can be seen from the central staircase and the upper floors of the main building, which was completed to the designs by Henry van de Velde in 1911 for the newly founded school of arts and crafts, into which the Staatliches Bauhaus moved only a few years later. The two photographs showing the spatial connection were taken during the ANNUAL SUMMÆRY in 2017 by Robert Elert. The *Tokyo Research Project – Display* exhibition, which we were hoping to discuss with you, is presented in Room 102, a small space on the first floor. Would it be possible to integrate your exhibition into the volume of the glass roof so that it could be seen inside the studio while also having an impact on the wider campus?

した。空間的なつながりを示す2枚の写真は、2017年の「ANNUAL SUMMÆRY」（バウハウス大学内の定期学術発表会）期間中にロバート・エーレルトが撮影したものです。1階にある小さな空間の102号室では、先に述べた「Two Houses」を含む「東京リサーチプロジェクト」の展覧会が開催されます。あなたの展覧会の展示デザインのアイディアと同じように、展示物をガラス屋根のボリュームに調和させることで、スタジオ内で展示物を鑑賞すると同時に、キャンパス全体に影響を与えることができるでしょうか。

　参加している学生と彼らの相互交流、そして展覧会の準備期間中の私たちの継続的な対話を含め、大学の教授間での協力をありがたく思います。また、展覧会の実施におけるハンナ・シュレッサー、そしてすべてのメンバーのサポートに感謝します。

敬具

I am grateful for the cooperation between our chairs; this includes the participating students and their exchange with one another, and our continuous dialogue during the preparation of your exhibition, without which I could not have written this letter. I would also like to thank Martin Pohl and Hanna Schlösser for their past and future support in the implementation of the exhibition.

Yours sincerely,

Summary

スタイルなき
アナザー・バウハウス
Another Bauhaus without style

伏見 唯
Yui FUSHIMI

　建築とインテリアが、一度にすべてデザインされることは、今や珍しい。まず家を買い、あるいは借り、そこに合うようにカーテンや絨毯を設え、家具や家電を置き、時には花や芸術作品で飾り付けていく。各住人が悩みながら、住宅と合うようにコーディネートしていくけれども、やはり別々に企画制作されてきたものをうまく調和させるのは簡単ではないことも多い。

　だがそもそも、建築や家具などがうまく調和しているというのはどういう状態なのか。意外と難しい。例えば、同じようなデ

Today, it is unusual for a home's architecture and interior design to be developed simultaneously. When people buy or rent a house, they hang up their curtains and place rugs on the floors to fit the house's design. They also arrange their furniture and appliances accordingly, and sometimes decorate with flowers or artwork. Although people try to beautify their homes in a suitable way, it is often difficult to coordinate the house's architecture with the interior simply because they were produced separately.

Thus, one must ask: What is the state of

ザインで統一されていれば、調和している
ということなのか。あるいは材質の統一か。
異なるもののなかにも相性のよいものがあ
るだろうし、一部を際立たせて別のものを
控えめに添えることでうまくいくこともあ
るだろう。むろん確たる調和などないが、
何らかの帰着点を求めて試行錯誤していく
のが、住まいを形作るうえでは堪らなく楽
しい。

ハウス・アム・ホルンに見る統一感

そうした全体の調和は、作り手側によっ
ても試みられ続けてきた。開校当初に「す
べての造形活動の最終目標は建築である」
という理念を掲げた、本展会場のバウハウ
スもその1つだろう。固有の領域の内部
に止まっていたという建築、絵画、彫刻な
どが、再び互いの垣根を越えて協調し合う
ことを理想としていた。実際にはバウハウ
スが各工房を総動員して作った建築は多く
はないけれども、会場近くにある初期のハ
ウス・アム・ホルン(1923)では、理念
の実践に努めていたことがよく伝わってく
る(注1)。

後のバウハウス建築の端緒といえる白い
箱のような外観の建築だが、それだけでは
なく内部もバウハウスの各専門の工房が担
い、建築と協調し合うように作られている。
例えば、キッチンには白い戸棚の上に、内
容物を示す大きな活字が添えられたテオ・
ボーグラーの白い陶器が置かれているさま
はしっくりくるうえ、内装の白さも含めて
衛生的な印象に仕立て上げたのだろう。中
央の居間には正方形が並べられたマルタ・
エルプスの絨毯、マルセル・ブロイアーの
直方体を積み重ねたような戸棚が置かれ、

harmony between a home's architecture and its furniture? Quite unexpectedly, this state is difficult to define. For example, if the two are unified according to the same design, does it mean that they are harmonious? Or should one use physical materials to unify them? Some things may go well together, creating a natural sense of harmony. Or, perhaps harmony may be created by highlighting some objects while downplaying others. Of course, there can be no definitive state of harmony, but it is irresistibly enjoyable to shape a home by trial and error and meet some higher aspiration.

A sense of unity in Haus Am Horn

Many designers have attempted to attain a sense of total harmony for a home. One such example is the Bauhaus in which this exhibition is held. At the Bauhaus's beginning, founders made this statement: "the ultimate goal of all artistic activity is the building"! At the time, architecture, painting, and sculpture had been delineated to their own domains. Thus, the school's ideal was to allow architects, painters, and sculptors to once again transcend artificial barriers and collaborate. Bauhaus designed only a few buildings in their workshops, but Haus am Horn (1923) — one of Bauhaus's early works, which is near this venue[1] — clearly demonstrated that the designers attempted to put Bauhaus's philosophy into practice.

The building's exterior looks like a white box, which characterizes Bauhaus's later architecture. The interior was created in Bauhaus's specialized workshops and was designed to coordinate with the building's body. For example, white ceramic wares, created by Theodor Bogler, were put on a white cupboard in the kitchen, showcasing large letters to describe what was inside.

正方形の部屋を反復した意匠が揃えられているように思える。工業化が進む時代に、進歩的な建築の仕事を示さなければいけなかったのだという (注2)。

1923年のバウハウス展で公開された後、この家は「白モルタルのサイコロ」「北極基地」「手術室」などと揶揄されたようだが (注3)、それは一言で切って捨てられてしまうほどに印象深い表現の統一が果たされた結果だとも言えるし、最終的に意義深いものだとも評価されたのは、極端な統一は「実験住宅」として有意義な姿だと判断されたためではないかと思う。さらにはその極端さのおかげで、バウハウスは著名な運動として知れ渡ったのだと考えられなくもない。

いずれにせよハウス・アム・ホルンでは、別々の作家によって作られているにもかかわらず、陶器、絨毯、家具、建築などを統一したデザインにまとめようとする熱量が明らかに大きい。初期バウハウスの理念の余熱のなかで築き上げられた結晶の1つだろう。

あるいはゾマーフェルト邸に見る百花繚乱

一方で、ハウス・アム・ホルンに先だって作られたゾマーフェルト邸（1920-21）は、同じ初期バウハウスの作品にもかかわらず、驚くほど似ていない。一見牧歌的な校倉造の構造と外観、表現主義的だと言われるギザギザの壁 (注4)、この頃からすでに積み木のようなデザインをするマルセル・ブロイアーのテーブル、正三角形などの基本図形をリズミカルに表現したヨースト・シュミットの玄関ドアや階段の手すりの彫刻、グリッドとともに不定形な図形が並ぶ

Each element aligns with the others perfectly and they (including the interior's whiteness) thus present a hygienic impression. The central living room features a square-patterned rug designed by Marta Erps and a cupboard by Marcel Breuer, which looks like a stack of squares. It seems as though the room's design was created by repeating the square pattern. This reflects the era's increasing industrialization, in response to which Bauhaus had to demonstrate progressive architectural work[2].

After the 1923 Bauhaus exhibition, Haus am Horn was ridiculed. Critics called it names such as "white mortar dice", "Arctic base", and "operating room"[3]. However, such criticism shows that house was, in fact, one complete and unified expression capable of leaving such a strong impression that critics could discard the house in one phase. However, in the long run, critics evaluated the house as significant and it may be the case that Haus am Horn's extreme unification was rightly judged as a significant form of the "experimental house". Moreover, it may be the case that the Bauhaus movement's extreme nature is what made Haus am Horn so well-known.

In fact, Haus Am Horn was the product of many different artists who were passionate about bringing pottery, carpets, furniture, and architecture together into one unified design. Haus am Horn is one of crystallized forms which demonstrated the remaining exuberance of the early Bauhaus movement.

A profusion of design elements in Haus Sommerfeld

On the other hand, Haus Sommerfeld (1920-1921), which was built before Haus am Horn (1923), is surprisingly distinct from Haus am Horn, even though both are early

乱張りのようなヨーゼフ・アルバースのステンドグラス、大小の三角形や四角形などのアップリケが取り付けられたデルテ・ヘルムによるカーテンなど。基本図形を出発点にしているところが共通しているが、異なる趣があり、それぞれが個性的な芸術作品の集合体のように見える。

　この家もまた、バウハウスの最初の理念を受けて、異なる専門の作家が共同で作品を作り上げる実践だったのであるが、2年後のハウス・アム・ホルンとデザインの方向性があまりに異なるのは、ウィリアム・モリス以来の手工芸を復興しようとする流れに影響されてバウハウスが誕生したため、最初の実践では手工芸的な建築が建てられたのだと言われている（注5）。時代遅れと見なされないように展覧会で進歩的な建築の全体像を見せなければいけなかった状況ではない。当初の理念通り、各分野の手工芸が発揮されることに力点を置き、その共同作業で純粋に建築を作り上げようとしていたのではないか。

　もちろん共作である以上、ゾマーフェルト邸においても共通のデザインを目指していた形跡はあるが、ハウス・アム・ホルンほど顕著ではない。いわばメディアの波にのれるような単純化された全体像をもてなかったために、後のバウハウスのイメージを形成していくほどの代表作にはなれなかった。

　しかし、むしろそのことによって、強い全体のイメージに1つひとつの家具や彫刻や建築の部位が回収されずに、自立して存在感を示しているように見えないだろうか。校倉造の骨格やギザギザの壁は、作家の想いが弾けるように表現されたヨース

Bauhaus buildings. Sommerfeld's structure and appearance are of an idyllic style combined with the joined-log structure. The house includes expressionistic notched walls4; Marcel Breuer's tables, which had already been designed like building blocks; an entrance door that rhythmically expressed a basic geometrical figure, such as an equilateral triangle, and a sculptured stair railing designed by Joost Schmidt; stained glass by Josef Albers, which looked like the pitching of irregular stones with grids; and curtains designed by Dörte Helm, which are attached with appliques, such as large and small triangles and quadrangles. Although both houses' designs are based on basic geometrical figures, they have different styles and each looks like it is a unique collection of artwork.

　Sommerfeld stands out in that professional creators worked on it collaboratively to practice a design philosophy based on the Bauhaus's original creed. However, the design policy differed greatly from that of Haus am Horn (1923) because Bauhaus's founding had been influenced by the trend of reviving handicraft work since William Morris (1834-96). Thus, the handicraft-oriented house (i.e., Sommerfeld) was built in the first phrase of practicing the Bauhaus philosophy[5]. As a result, the 1923 exhibition did not need to show the progressiveness of the whole architecture so that the house would not be considered old-fashioned. As originally envisioned, the Sommerfeld focused on displaying the handicraft work of various fields, aiming to create a purely architectural structure through collaboration.

　Because Haus Sommerfeld was the result of artistic collaboration, Sommerfeld

ト・シュミットの彫刻を従属させるほどに
強い印象を与えているわけではない。その
ためこの家を、「白モルタルのサイコロ」
のような建築の外観に代表させて一言で表
現するのは難しい。建築、絵画、彫刻など
がそれぞれに自立的に振る舞いながらも干
渉し、結果的に名なしの全体像を築いてい
く道もまた、バウハウスの当初の理念に則
していたはずだ。この道を進めば、声の大
きい建築宣言だったヴァルター・グロピウ
スのインターナショナル・スタイルとは異
なる、パウル・クレーやヴァシリー・カン
ディンスキーの絵、オスカー・シュレンマー
の演出、ラスロ・モホリ＝ナギの光の扱い
などの諸芸術が建築と対等か、それ以上の
存在として組み込まれた、まったく想像も
つかないアナザー・バウハウスが生まれた
かもしれない。見てみたかった。

bears signs that it was built based on one common design. However, this fact is not as prominent as it is with Haus am Horn. Because the Sommerfeld did not have a simplified, comprehensive image that could easily be influenced by the media, it did not become a representative work that would later shape Bauhaus's reputation.

However, it may seem as if Sommerfeld's strong overall image does not adequately capture the unity of the individual furniture pieces, sculptures, and architecture, but rather that each piece is showcased independently. Indeed, the framework of the joined-log structure style and the jagged walls do not give a strong impression capable of subordinating Joost Schmidt's sculptures (an artist who passionately expressed his thoughts) to the main structure. Therefore, unlike Haus am Horn, it

ハウス・アム・ホルン（ワイマール）
Haus am Horn, Weimar

ハウス・アム・ホルンのキッチン
Kitchen in Haus am Horn

統一されずに連鎖する有り様の探求

　今でもなお、できるだけ同じようなデザインのものを家に置いていくことがインテリアの秘訣なのかもしれない。バウハウスやフランク・ロイド・ライトまでいかなくても、うまく統一されたものには確かに惹かれる。しかし、実際にはそれを徹底するのは難しいだろう。好みのオーディオ、テーブル、食器、あるいは炊飯器、本棚、クッション、パソコン。到底統一できそうにない。せいぜい、例えば木調のものに揃えるくらいのことしかできず、結果、木目プリントの電化製品などが出てくる。あるいはしびれを切らしたDIYも流行する。時には、そこまでして揃えたいか、という気分になる。

　ゾマーフェルト邸のように、強い全体像がなくとも、個々のものがそれぞれに自立しながらも連鎖しながら全体を築いていくようにはできないだろうか。そこで求められるのは、異なるものが共存するときの連鎖の有り様に対する知見なのではないか。あるいは連鎖しやすいものづくりの方法であろう。本展の用語でいえば、前者が「Synesthesia Scenery」、後者が「Non-scale materiality」の概念に近い。1つひとつは個別に企画されてつくられた事物であっても、連鎖するように作る工夫がなされていれば、強いデザインとコンセプトで統御しなくても、一定の調和を生み出してくれるのではないか。

　スタイルなき時代に生きるクリエイターが自身の専門を越境して融合を密かに果たすために、連鎖の有り様を探求した末に敷衍させる不可視のコードを待ち望んでいる。アナザー・バウハウスを求めて。

is difficult to describe Sommerfeld in one phrase by invoking an architectural phrase such as "white mortar dice". The way architecture, painting, and sculpture are showcased independently while simultaneously interacting with each other, resulted in a kind of ambiguous picture, which may have aligned with Bauhaus's original philosophy as well. Bauhaus's quest regarding such a notion may have given rise to the utterly unimaginable name, "Another Bauhaus", branding it quite unlike the loud architectural declarations of International Style by Walter Gropius, art such as the paintings of Paul Klee and Wassily Kandinsky, the renderings of Oskar Schlemmer, or the expression of light by László Moholy-Nagy, which were all deemed equal to—or more than architecture. If that had happened, what would it have been?

A quest for how things should be connected while foregoing unification

　Like Bauhaus's philosophy, the key to successful interior design may still be arranging as many similar elements as possible. We are often attracted to well-unified architecture, even if the thoroughness of unification does not quite reach the level of Bauhaus or Frank Lloyd Wright. In practice, however, it would truly be difficult to thoroughly integrate diverse elements of interior design. Your favorite audio device, table, tableware, rice cooker, bookcase, cushion, and computer. There is no way we could completely unify each individual object. At best, a unified design could be reached by using wood-like products and, as a result, wood-printed electrical appliances would be launched. Yet, there are those who cannot tolerate any superficial uniformity of design; thus, they

ゾマーフェルト邸（ベルリン）
Sommerfeld House, Berlin

ゾマーフェルト邸のホール
Hall in Sommerfeld House

stick with DIY. At times, you may even wonder whether you want to go that far and acquiesce to making the design uniform.

Even without a strong vision, like that of Haus Sommerfeld, is it possible to create a design in which each object expresses its own unique design features, but is nonetheless linked to the others? What is clearly needed here is the knowledge of how different objects can be linked to one another when they coexist. Or, perhaps, what is needed is knowledge of composition so that each object interacts effortlessly. In this exhibition's terminology, the former is close to the "synesthesia scenery" concept, while the latter is close to the "no-scale material" concept. Even if each design element were individually planned and created to interact, then one could conceivably create a certain degree of harmony without being strongly controlled by the demand to integrate designs and concepts.

For creators, who live in an era of stylelessness, to cross their professional boundaries and achieve fusion without conspicuousness, they must leverage the invisible codes to amplify such linkage after exploring the nature of composition, thus seeking "Another Bauhaus".

■注釈
注1 Adolf Meyer, 1925. EIN VERSUCHSHAUS DES BAUHAUSES IN WEIMAR（アドルフ・マイヤー編、貞包博幸訳『新装版 バウハウス叢書3 バウハウスの実験住宅』、中央公論美術出版、1925年）。
注2 杉本俊多『バウハウス その建築造形理念』、鹿島出版会、1979年。
注3 Magdalena Droste, 2001. bauhaus 1919-1933. Köln: TASCHEN GmbH
注4 注3と同書。
注5 注2と同書。

■ NOTES
1. Adolf Meyer, 1925. EIN VERSUCHSHAUS DES BAUHAUSES IN WEIMAR
2. Toshimasa SUGIMOTO, 1979. Bauhaus Sono Kenchiku Zokei Rinen. Tokyo: KAJIMA INSTITUTE PUBLISHING.
3. Magdalena Droste, 2001. bauhaus 1919-1933. Köln: TASCHEN GmbH.
4. ibid.
5. See NOTE 2

18

Objects

18の
オブジェクト

ここに並べられた
日本の近現代建築の断片たちは、
今では見えにくくなった
デザインの伏流を示します。
唯一の古代からの事例が、
そのか細くも長い系統を支持しています。

The pieces of
Japanese modern architecture
lined up here show the undercurrent of
design that is now hard to see.
The only ancient case supports
the slender but long lineage.

1. 人間が作った木のなかに隠し込まれた鉄

Hidden Steel in the Man-made Tree

法隆寺五重塔 鍛造釘（レプリカ）
制作／河野純也　2020年
Replicas of forged nails used for the Pagoda in Horyuji (Horyu Temple),
crafted by Junya KAWANO, 2020

b

法隆寺五重塔 断面図
写真／©佐竹敦　鍛造釘X線写真制作／渡邊大志研究室
The section of the five-storied pagoda in Horyuji, photo©Atsushi SATAKE,
X-ray photo of forged nails by Taishi WATANABE Lab.

2. 様々な材料で作られる道具の世界
World of Tools

道具曼陀羅絵図
写真／©GKデザイングループ　2006年
Dougu World Mandala,
©GK Design Group, 2006

道具寺道具村イメージ図
写真／©GKデザイングループ　2006年
The Master Plan for Dougu Temple & Dougu Village,
©GK Design Group, 2006

3. 紙とガラスのスクリーン
Paper Glass Screen

A邸障子とステンドグラス
設計／北園徹　写真／©石黒守
Shoji and Stained Glass in A House designed by Toru KITAZONO,
photo© Mamoru ISHIGURO

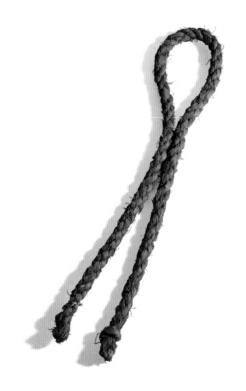

山笠 舁き縄
Carrying Rope for Yamakasa floats

g

山笠 建設風景
写真／©博多祇園山笠振興会
A building scene of Yamakasa floats,
photo©Hakata Gion Yamakasa
Promotion Association

h

博多祇園山笠 お祭り風景
写真／©博多祇園山笠振興会
A parade scene of Hakata Gion Yamakasa,
photo©Hakata Gion Yamakasa
Promotion Association

5. 縄で固定された木からこぼれる光
Light from Roped Woods

山笠の台座を基にした照明
写真／©高木正三郎

The wooden structure of Yamakasa floats,
photo©Shozaburo TAKAKI

山笠の木組構造
写真／©高木正三郎

Light from the base of Yamakasa floats,
photo©Shozaburo TAKAKI

6. 陶磁の壁掛け
Ceramic Tapestry

綿業会館 ラウンジのタイルタペストリー（大阪府）　1931年竣工
設計／渡辺節　写真／©株式会社渡辺建築事務所
Tile tapestry of the lounge in Cotton Industry Hall, Osaka,
built in 1931, designed by Setsu WATANABE, photo©TOKYO WATANABE
ARCHITECTS & ASSOCIATES

世界平和記念聖堂 鐘塔のレンガタペストリー（広島県）　1954年竣工
設計／村野藤吾　写真／©カトリック広島司教館
Brick Tapestry of the Bell Tower in Memorial Cathedral for World Peace, Hiroshima
built in 1954, designed by Togo MURANO,
photo©Catholic Hiroshima Bishop's Museum

8. 捻られた工業製品の鉄
Twisted Ready-made Steel

所沢聖地霊園 鋼材の門扉（埼玉県所沢市）　1973年竣工
設計／池原義郎　写真／©加藤詞史
Steel Bar Gate, Tokorozawa Seichi Cemetery,
designed by Yoshiro IKEHARA in 1973,
Tokorozawa City, Saitama pref., Japan, photo©Kotofumi KATO

ペーパーナイフと文鎮
設計／池原義郎　写真／©加藤詞史
Paper Knife & Paper Weight,designed by Yoshiro IKEHARA,
photo© Kotofumi KATO

「星をとる男」(レプリカ)
設計／池原義郎　制作／加藤詞史　写真／©加藤詞史
"Man Catching Star & Stargazer" (replica),
designed by Yoshiro IKEHARA, crafted by Kotofumi KATO, photo©Kotofumi KATO

バティックギャラリー 鋼板の庇
設計／加藤詞史　写真／©加藤詞史
Steel Plate Canopy, Batik Gallery designed by Kotofumi KATO,
photo © Kotofumi KATO

11. ラーニング・フロム・フィンランディア
Learning from Finlandia

「Learning from Finlandia」
作画／渡邊大志

"Learning from Finlandia", Drawing by
Taishi WATANABE

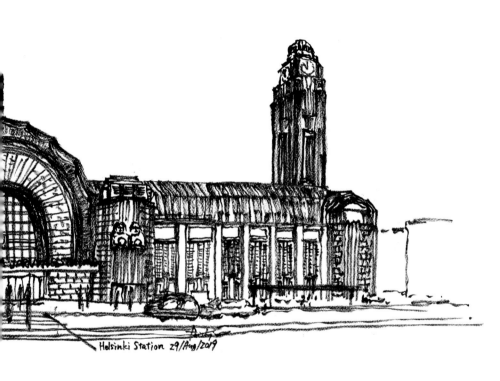

Helsinki Station 29/Aug/2019

q

「Object」
コラージュ／渡邊大志研究室
"Object", collage by Taishi WATANABE Lab.

r

「Light」
コラージュ／渡邊大志研究室
"Light", collage by Taishi WATANABE Lab.

18のオブジェクト解説
Description of 18 Objects

1. 人間が作った木のなかに 隠し込まれた鉄（a-b）

日本の多くの古い建築は複雑に木が組み立てられた木造のように見えますが、実際には木以外の材料も使われている場合があります。現存する日本最古の木造建築である法隆寺もそのうちの1つです。607年に建てられた五重塔は当時の超高層建築でした。高さ31.5mの塔には、職人が人力で打った無数の鍛造釘が発見されています。それらは全て微妙に異なる形状をしています。いずれも外から見えないように、桙（棟から軒先を支える大梁に渡す小梁）、裳階板掛（軒下壁面に付いた庇状構造物の横材）、天井廻縁（天井と壁面が接する縁）などに隠し釘として使われました。レントゲン写真では、屋根の横材と縦材は鍛造釘によって留められています。さらに、桙の上に置かれた瓦を止めるための横材も同様、鍛造釘によって留められています。日本は地震が多いことで有名ですが、このような鉄の彫刻とも言える鍛造釘が耐震の木材超高層ビルを実現させたのです。

2. 様々な材料で作られる 道具の世界（c-d）

私たちの日常生活は、数えきれないほどの道具によって支えられています。「道具寺道具村構想」は、日本のインダストリアルデザイナーとして国際的に活躍した栄久庵憲司（1929-2015）によるものです。ものづくりは人間の

1. Hidden Steel in the Man-made Tree（a-b）

Many old buildings in Japan look like intricately assembled pure wooden structures, but in fact, other materials are used. Horyuji (Horyu Temple), one of the oldest existing wooden buildings in Japan, is an example. The five-storied pagoda built in 607 was a skyscraper of the time. In constructing the Pagoda, with a height of 31.5 m, countless craftsmen forged nails that holding some of the structure together are found inside. The nails were made into slightly different shapes. They are hidden in the structures such as the rafter (which passes from the ridge to the girder), Mokoshi-Itagake (literally "skirt story" or "cuff story", is a decorative pent roof surrounding a building below the true roof), and the crown molding (joint edge of wall and ceiling). Therefore none of the nails could be seen from outside. You can find examples on the X-ray photo of forged nails. The horizontal and vertical components of the roof are fastened with forged nails. A crosspiece is fastened on a rafter with a forged nail to fix the roof tile. Even though in a country famous for frequent earthquakes like Japan, such forged nails, which shall be called iron sculptures, have made it possible to create an earthquake-resistant high-rise architecture.

2. World of Tools（c-d）

Our daily lives are supported by countless tools. "The Master plan for Dougu Temple and Dougu Village" was designed by Kenji EKUAN

文化・文明を支える基礎として永い歴史を刻んできました。しかし、今日のような物質的な豊かさの陰には、その代償として地球環境の危機、精神文化の衰退、コミュニティ社会の崩壊など多くの課題が生み出されています。榮久庵憲司は、今こそデザイナーというものづくりの立場から、ものをめぐる文化、文明のあり方を問い直す必要があるのではないかとこの構想に至りました。自身が僧侶でもある栄久庵は、大量生産、大量消費されるものの世界にも「輪廻」があると考えます。そして、工業力をもってできる道具に美しさをあたえる生業としての職業を確立し、「美の民主化」を目指しました。一部の特権階級のみならず、一般の庶民の人々も使える美しい道具作りを進め、それは同時に「ものづくりによるひとづくり」そのものでもありました。

「道具曼荼羅」は、人と道具の関係によって構築される世界を構造的に表現したマトリックスです。中心の円には人びとの心の象徴として、道具千手観音像を配置し、それを囲む円ごとに私たちの生活を取り巻く様々な道具が類型されています。

「道具寺道具村構想」絵図は、道具寺を中心に、道具大学、道具工房、道具リサイクルセンター、道具墓地、道具劇場、道具博物館など多彩な施設を配置し、デザインの理想郷ともいえる村づくり構想となっています。

3. 紙とガラスのスクリーン (e)

障子とステンドグラスを1枚に収めたこの写真は、日本の木造住宅である「A邸」の1室で撮影されました。「A邸」は、側道に小川の流れる通りに面した約530㎡ある敷地に建ち、2019年に竣工しました。デザイナーは、北園徹（1965-）です。障子は日本で屏風とともに古くから用いられる空間装置です。それは空間を隔てることもつなぐこともできます。細い木組の格子に和紙と呼ばれる光を透かす薄い

(1929-2015), an international industrial designer in Japan. Manufacturing has a long history as a foundation that supports human culture and civilization. However, the material wealth like today made a lot of problems in return such as the crisis of the global environment, the decline of spiritual culture, and the collapse of community society. Kenji EKUAN created the concept, thinking that now is the time to need for designer to reconsider about the Manufacturing culture and civilization. Ekuan, who is also a monk himself, thought that even in a world of mass production and mass consumption, there was also a "transmigration". Then, he established the occupation that gives beauty to tools made with industrial power and aimed at "democratized beauty". The aim was to create beautiful tools that could be used not only by some privileged classes but also by ordinary people. At the same time, it was also "human development through manufacturing". "Dougu World Mandala" is a matrix that structurally expresses the world constructed by the relationship between human and tools. In the center circle is a Statue of Thousand-Armed Dougu Kannon as a symbol of people's hearts, and various tools surrounding our life are typified by the circle surrounding center. "The Master plan for Dougu Temple and Dougu Village" is a village developmant concept as an ideal home for design, with a variety of facilities around Dougu temple including a Dougu university, Dougu workshop, Dougu recycling center, Dougu graveyard, Dougu theater, Dougu museum, etc.

3. Paper Glass Screen (e)

The photo below capturing shoji and stained glass within one view was taken in a room within a Japanese wooden house called "A House". "A House" was completed in 2019 on a 530 square meter site, facing a street where a stream runs beside. The designer was Toru KITAZONO (1965–). Shoji is a spatial device, along with folding screens, which has long been used in Japan. It

紙が貼り付けられており、特定の場所に固定されずに動かすことができます。一方、日本におけるステンドグラスは近代以降の教会や洋館を中心に普及しました。「A邸」のステンドグラスは、透過度の異なる2種類の磨りガラスと色付きの板ガラスで構成されます。障子を通した淡い光の下に、ステンドグラスに描かれた庭とその奥に見える庭の虚実2つの庭によって、面であるスクリーンに奥行きが与えられています。

4. 動く木造の山車 (f-g-h)

　古代にすでに完成していた日本の木組みの技術は、日本中で受け継がれています。博多祇園山笠もその1つです。山笠は、木によって組まれた骨格に人形を飾り付けた山車で、1年に1度、7月ごろに、この塔状の山車が市民に引かれて町中を駆け巡ります。現存する日本最古の木造建築とされる法隆寺には、加工した木を組み合わせた塔が隠し釘によって支えられていました。しかしこの高さ約10-15mの山笠の土台に釘は一切使われず、木材は縄のみで固定されています。山笠の山車は、熟練した職人の手によって作られるのではなく、普段は他の仕事をしている市民たちによって毎年製作されます。縄の扱いには特殊な技術は必要なく、結び方さえ覚えていれば、誰にでも等しく作ることができます。その縄は、ある時は山笠に使われる木を清めるための儀式の道具になり、祭りの最中は、山笠と担ぎ手をつなぐための重要なアイテムとなります。それは担ぎ手の足がもつれた時、舁き縄にしがみつくことで転倒を回避する命綱です。

5. 縄で固定された 木からこぼれる光 (i)

　山笠の土台の木組みとそれを支える縄の結びを転用したシェードの光です。福岡市にある櫛田神社の北神門の敷地に計画中のホールのため

can separate or connect spaces. The Shoji, a thin wooden lattice, pasted with thin translucent paper (called Washi or Japanese paper), can move freely without being fixed to a specific place. On the other hand, the trend of stained glass in Japan has mainly spread through churches and western-style buildings since the modern age. The stained glass of "A House" is composed of two types of frosted glass with different transmittance and one kind of colored flat glass. Under the faint light through the shoji screen, the imaginary garden on the stained glass along with the real garden behind it gives depth to the plane experienced in the picture below.

4. Mobile Wooden Float (f-g-h)

　The technology of Japanese timber frame was completed in ancient times, and then it has been inherited throughout Japan. "Hakata Gion Yamakasa" is one of them. Yamakasa is a kind of wooden frame float decorated with dolls. Once a year, around July, this kind of tower-shaped float is carried by citizens and runs around the town. At Horyuji, which is the oldest existing wooden building in Japan, the wooden frame pagoda is supported with hidden nails. However, no nails are used at the base part of the 10-15m high Yamakasa. Here the woods are fixed with only ropes. The Yamakasa is not made by skilled craftsmen but annually by citizens who have their own careers. No special skills are needed to handle the rope, and anyone who can remember the way of tying can make the same Yamakasa. The rope sometimes is used as a ritual tool to purify the woods of Yamakasa, but during the festival, it is an important item to connect the Yamakasa to the bearers. It is a lifeline that avoids falling down when the bearer's legs are tangled.

5. Light from Roped Woods (i)

　It is light from the sunshade that uses the wood frame of the base of Yamakasa and knot of the rope that supports it. It was designed in a hall

にデザインされました。博多祇園山笠は、この櫛田神社の奉納行事です。デザイナーは、高木正三郎（1969-）です。櫛田神社の境内の一部と言える敷地のため、山笠の土台をアレンジしたデザインが考えられました。山笠台の木と麻縄による構造は、脚が折れることを縄が防ぎ、かつ、台全体のねじれを受け止めて逃がすための緩衝材となるというものです。その力学的な原理は、水を含んで収縮性を高めた縄の束を台の足に対角線状に結びつけ、それらを交点で編み込むことによります。この原理を逆に解きほぐすようにして、束になった縄を分割し、編み込みを増やしていくことで、デザインにバリエーションが生まれます。この工夫は、700年前から博多の人々が脈々と受け継いできた知恵なのです。

6. 陶磁の壁掛け（j）

矩形の陶磁器の集合が6m程の高さを覆っています。これは、大阪府に建つ綿業会館の談話室にあります。綿業会館は、綿業界の交流のための施設として1931年に建設されました。デザイナーは、渡辺節（1884-1967）です。渡辺は世界平和記念聖堂をデザインした村野の師としても知られています。ここでは5種類の浮き彫りの陶磁器が使われています。同じ製法でも、緑、白、茶の3色の鉛釉の塗り方の変化によって全てが異なる表情をしています。さらに、渡辺が現場で1枚1枚異なる陶磁器のコンビネーションを自ら考えて全体を仕上げました。この陶磁器は、泰山タイルと呼ばれ、池田泰山という職人が1917年に設立した京都の製陶所で作られたものです。製陶所では渡辺の意向に合わせて、素地土の調整から窯の焼成法の開発まで行われました。当時は既に機械による大量生産が可能であり、多くの工業製品タイルが市場に出回っていましたが、池田は単なる建築の仕上げ材としてでは無く美術品としてタイルを製造しました。

planed on the site next to the north gate of Kushida Shrine in Fukuoka City. Hakata Gion Yamakasa is a dedication event of Kushida Shrine. The designer is Shozaburo TAKAKI (1969–). Because the site is a part of the Kushida Shrine's territory, the design of the base of Yamakasa was specially arranged. The hemp rope at Yamakasa base is designed to prevent its base stand from breaking, and also work as a cushioning to catch and release the entire torsion of the base.

The mechanical principle is working like that a bundle of rope, which absorbs water to be enhanced contractility, is tied diagonally to the feet of the table and woven at the intersection. Takaki creates variations in the design by unravelling this principle in reverse, such as dividing the bundle of ropes and increasing the number of braids. This ingenuity is the wisdom that Hakata people have inherited since 700 years ago.

6. Ceramic Tapestry （j）

There are clusters of quadrilateral ceramics that cover a height of about 6m. They are in the lounge of the Cotton Industry Hall in Osaka Prefecture. The Cotton Industry Hall was built in 1931 as a facility for the communication of the cotton industry. The designer was Setsu WATANABE (1884-1967). Watanabe is also known as the teacher of Togo MURANO, who designed Memorial Cathedral for World Peace in Hiroshima. Five types of embossed ceramics are used here. Although produced in the same manufacturing method, each ceramic looks different depending on how the three colors of the lead glaze of green, white, and brown are applied. Watanabe considered the combination of different ceramics one by one on the site and finished the whole composition by himself. This ceramic configuration is called the Taizan tile, and it was made at a pottery factory in Kyoto, founded in 1917 by a craftsman named Taizan IKEDA. The pottery factory performed operations from base

7. ヒロシマの土（k）

　このフランス積みされたモルタルレンガは、被爆した広島の土を用いたものです。「Hiroshima-clay」が「世界平和記念聖堂」の塔45mを形作っています。これは第2次世界大戦の終りまでの禁教と第2次世界大戦の原爆投下の2つの苦しい経験から、1954年に再建されました。デザイナーである村野藤吾（1891-1984）はこの世界平和記念聖堂を造る際、30万個ものレンガの製作を外注しませんでした。意図的に叩きの荒いブロックを現場で職人に手作りさせたのです。それぞれのレンガは、重量を軽くするために中抜きになっています。彼の指示により25mmほどの突起を付けながら積まれた広島の土は、地球が強く侵食を受けた時の経過と人為性を強調します。この突起は偶然に生まれたものではなく、デザイン図が存在し、その大きさは縦2m60cm横82cmに及んだといいます。

8. 捻られた工業製品の鉄（I）

　捻られた鉄の平板の連続によって作られた美しい造形物は、規格化された工業製品から固有のデザインが生まれる可能性を最も端的に示しています。それは所沢聖地霊園の入り口にあります。デザイナーは池原義郎（1928-2017）です。池原は建築と建築以外のものを区別なくデザインすることができた、日本では極めて稀有な建築家でした。この鉄の彫刻は実際には墓地のメインエントランスの門扉であり、約1mの間隔で1回転ねじられた幅120mm、厚さ4.5mmの鋼板が25mほど伸びています。所沢聖地霊園が竣工した1970年代は、工業化された建築部品の組み合わせによって工場生産によるプレハブ建築が作られ始めた時代でした。日本の建築構法の第一人者である内田祥哉は、この池原の門扉のデザインを見て、工業化された建築部品を用いた建築デザインが生む豊かさ

soil adjustments to the development of kiln firing methods, according to the request of clients. At that time, mass production by machine was already possible and many industrial tiles were on the market, but Ikeda manufactured tiles as artwork, not just as finishing materials for architecture.

7. Stacked Hiroshima-clay（k）

　The Flemish bond mortar bricks here are made of bombed earth from Hiroshima, and the "Hiroshima-clay" bricks built up the 45m tower of the "Memorial Cathedral for World Peace". Suffering from two painful experiences, the ban on Christianity, and the atomic bombing by the end of World War II, the Cathedral was rebuilt in 1954. Instead of outsourcing the production of 300,000 bricks for the construction of the cathedral, designer Togo MURANO (1891-1984) asked the workers to make the intentionally rough bricks by hand on the site. Each brick is hollowed out to reduce weight. Suggested by Murano, Hiroshima-clay, with a protrusion of about 25 mm, emphasizes its artificiality the passage when the earth was strongly eroded. The protrusions were produced by design, instead of by accident, and reached a size of 2m and 60cm long and 82cm wide.

8. Twisted Ready-made Steel（I）

　The beautiful objects created by the series of twisted iron bars extremely clearly show the potential for unique designs to emerge from standardized industrial products. The iron object locates at the entrance of Tokorozawa Seichi Cemetery. The designer is Yoshiro IKEHARA (1928-2017). Ikehara was a rare architect in Japan who was able to design both architecture and non-architecture without distinguishing them. This iron sculpture is actually the gate of cemetery's main entrance, with a steel plate (120mm wide and 4.5mm thick) twisted once at about 1m intervals, extending about 25m. The

に気づくと同時に、プレハブ時代においても建築家が持つデザインの職能の重要性が依然として存在することを当時の建築雑誌に記録しています。

9. 手作りで加工された金属 (m-n)

池原義郎は異なるスケールのものを同一の感性と密度でデザインすることができました。「星をとる男と深海魚」は、池原自身によってデザインされた遊園地の道に掛けられたアーチの上に立つ彫刻です。これはカール・ミレスそのものへのオマージュであり、虹に登って天空の星を取ろうとする男を、その足元でスターゲイザーと命名された魚が見つめています。他にも池原は、長さ 120mm のペーパーナイフや直径約 80mm のペーパーウエイト、さらには彼が教鞭をとった早稲田大学の記念メダルなども建築を扱うのと同じような手つきでデザインしました。むしろ、建築がこれらのデザインと同じような手つきでデザインされていると言うべきかもしれません。池原のデザインはスケールや分野による制約を受けない日本では稀なものでした。

10. 浮遊する鉄 (o)

この鉄の造形物は 1 枚の鉄板が折り紙のように折り曲げられて作られています。2006 年に建てられたジャワ更紗を飾る「バティックギャラリー」のためにデザインされました。デザイナーは、加藤詞史（1964-）です。加藤は10 年以上に渡って、池原義郎の下で協働しました。池原のペーパーナイフを思わせるこの繊細な鉄の造形物は、厚さ 3.2mm の鋼板を幅2,220mm、奥行き 820mm、高さ 260mm にプレス形成して作られました。それは彫刻でありながら、階段上に浮かぶキャノピーでもあります。同様の方法で作られたもう 1 つのものは、ギャラリーのエントランス上部に浮かべられて

Tokorozawa Seichi Cemetery was completed in the 1970s when factory-built prefabricated buildings which are the combination of industrialized building components came out. Looking at the design of the gate by Ikehara, Yoshichika UCHIDA, a leading person of Japanese building construction methods, recorded in the architectural magazine at that time that he realized the richness of architectural design using industrialized building components and noticed the importance of architects' design skills still exists during the prefab era.

9. Hand-made Metal (m-n)

Yoshiro IKEHARA was able to design different scales with the same sensitivity and density. "*Man Catching Star & Stargazer* " is a sculpture that stands on an arch along the path of an amusement park designed by Ikehara himself. This is a tribute to Carl MILLES and a man trying to take a star in the sky is stared by a deep-sea fish named Stargazer at his feet. Ikehara also designed a 120 mm long paper knife, a paper weight with a diameter of about 80 mm, and a commemorative medal at Waseda University, where he taught, in the way he handles architecture. Or, may the architecture is designed like the way he handles these designs. Ikehara's designs were rare in Japan, not restricted by scale or field.

10. Floating Steel (o)

Designed for the 2006 "Batik Gallery", the exhibition site of the Java Chintz, this iron object is made by folding a single iron plate with the concept of origami. The designer was Kotofumi KATO (1964-). Kato has been working with Yoshiro IKEHARA for over ten years. Reminding people of Ikehara's paper knife, this delicate iron object was made by pressing a 3.2mm thick steel plate to 2,220mm in width, 820mm in-depth, and 260mm in height. It is a sculpture, but also a canopy floating above the steps. Another awning

います。これらの鉄の彫刻は、そのシェイプを際立たせるために壁面から距離をおくことで影がきれいに落ちるように意図されています。前面から落ちる枝葉の影とともに、背後にあるウロコ張りされた杉板に落ちる映像となった「美」がそこにあります。

11. ラーニング・フロム・フィンランディア（p-q-r）

　これらの作品は、渡邊大志が現地を訪れた際に描いたスケッチをもとに作られました。1つ目はヘルシンキ中央駅のスケッチです。2つ目は「Object」という名前のコラージュ作品、最後は「Light」というコラージュ作品です。2つのコラージュ作品の題材は以下の通りです。

コラージュ「Object」の題材
（アルファベット順）

　アアルト自邸外観、文化会館用のアアルト煉瓦、アアルトアトリエ外観、アアルトアトリエの内部空間、アアルトアトリエの階段、アアルトの墓、鳥、アルクティクム博物館 ボートの展示品、アルクティクム博物館の展示品、アルクティクム博物館 サーミ人の道具の展示品、アルクティクム博物館 サーミ人の民族服の展示品、フィンランド国立博物館 熊の石像、サーロイネンのレンガ倉庫、エリアス・レンロットの記念碑、フィンランディアホール外観、エスポーボスマルム 原初の家、フィスカース川の水、ガッレン＝カッレラ邸外観、ガッレン＝カッレラ邸の内部空間、ノールマルックの馬、イッタラガラス工場、アテネウム美術館 カレワラの部屋、カレオ教会、キアズマの階段、コエタロの中庭、コエタロのタイル、文化会館、フィンランディアホールからの風景、ラッピアホール外観、ラッピアホールの内部空間、ラッピアホールのロビー、ラッピアホールの階段、ミュールマキ教会外観、フィンランド国立博物館、ノー

made in the same way floats above the gallery entrance. These iron sculptures, to accurate their shapes, are intended to cast delicate shadows while being placed at a distance from the wall. The "beauty" emerges where the shadows of the branches and leaves fall from the casted shadow, overlapping with the shadow of the iron sculpture on the Shingles cedar siding.

11. Learning from Finlandia（p-q-r）

　These pictures were made of the sketches that Taishi WATANABE drew while visiting the field. The first one is the sketch of Helsinki Central Station. The second one is the collage named "Object". The last one is the collage named "Light". The subjects of two collages are as follows;

Object

　Object (A to Z) : Aalto House Exterior, Aalto Studio Brick for Kulttuuritalo, Aalto Studio Exterior, Aalto Studio Interior, Aalto Studio Stairs, Aalto's Tomb, Bird, Arktikum Boat Exhibit, Arktikum Exhibit, Arktikum Saami Goods Exhibit, Arktikum Saami People Dress Exhibit, Bear Statue in Finland National Museum, Brick Warehouse in Saaroinen, Elias Lönnrot Monument, Finlandia Hall Exterior, The First House in Espoo Bosmalm, Fiskars River Water, Gallen-Kallela House Exterior, Gallen-Kallela House Interior, Noormarkku Horse, Iittala Glass Factory, Kalevala Room in Ateneum Art Museum, Kallion Kirkko, Kiasma Stairs, Koetalo Courtyard, Koetalo Tiles, Kulttuuritalo, Landscape from Finlandia Hall, Lappia-talo Exterior, Lappia-talo Interior, Lappia-talo Lobby, Lappia-talo Stairs, Myyrmaki Church Exterior, National Museum of Finland, Noormarkku Kolin Sauna, Noormarkku Power Canal, Olari Church Exterior, Olari Church Interior, Pakila Church Ceiling, Pakila Church Interior, Petäjävesi Old Church Saint Statue, Petajavesi Old Church Joint Details, Port of Helsinki, Porvoo Cathedral, Porvoo House, Romulus and Remus by Oiva Toikka,

ルマルックのコリンサウナ、ノールマルックの動力運河、オラリ教会外観、オラリ教会の内部空間、パキラ教会の天井、パキラ教会の内部空間、ペタヤヴェシの古い教会の聖人像、ペタヤヴェシの古い教会の接合部、ヘルシンキ港、ポルヴォー大聖堂、ポルヴォーの家、オイバ・トイッカのロームルスとレムス像、ロヴァニエミ市立図書館と市庁舎外観、ロヴァニエミ市立図書館の内部空間、サーリネンのビルとアアルトのアカデミア書店、サウナサーリ、シベリウスの記念碑、ワイナミョイネンの銅像、スオメンリンナ島の家、スオメンリンナ島の村、スオメリンナ島の煉瓦の家、タンメルコスキ、タンペレの水門、タピオラの教会、タピオラの教会の婦人、タピオラの森、タピオラのヘイキントリ、タピオラ図書館の子供用椅子、タピオラの霊園、タピオラの風景、トゥルク大聖堂、トゥルクの家、生神女就寝大聖堂、ヴァニオラ、ヘルシンキ発タリン行きヴァイキングライン、ヴァリラ地区、マイレア邸のディテール、マイレア邸の玄関、マイレア邸の階段

コラージュ「Light」の題材
（アルファベット順）

アアルトホール、アアルトの家、アアルトミュージアム、アアルトアトリエの内部空間、アアルトカフェ、フィンランディアホール、フィンランディアホールの内部空間、フィスカース川の水、森、ヘルシンキ教会、ヘルシンキ港、カンピ教会、キアズマ、コエタロ、ラップランドハウス、オラリ教会、パキラ教会、ペタヤヴェシの古い教会、ポルヴォー大聖堂、鉄鋼業者協同組合ビル、ロヴァニエミ市庁舎と図書館、ロヴァニエミ図書館、セイナッツァロ、ヘルシンキ市電力会社ビル、タンペレ大聖堂、タピオラ、タピオラ教会、タピオラ墓地、タピオラホール、タピオラホールのトップライト、タピオラのショッピングセンター、トゥルク大聖堂、マイレア邸

Rovaniemi City Library and Town Hall Exterior, Rovaniemi Library Interior, Saarinen's Building and Aalto's Akateeminen Kirjakauppa, Saunasaari, Sibelius Monument, Statue of Väinämöinen, Suomenlinna House, Suomenlinna Village, Suomenlinna Brick House, Tammerkoski, Tampere Water Gate, Tapiola Church, Tapiola Church Lady, Tapiola Forest, Tapiola Heikintori, Tapiola Library Child Chairs, Tapiola Cemetory, Tapiola Landscape, Turku Cathedral, Turku House, Uspenski Cathedral, Vainiola, Viking Line Helsinki to Tallinn, Vallila District, Villa Mairea Details, Villa Mairea Entrance, Villa Mairea Stairs.

Light

Light (A to Z) : Aalto Hall, Aalto House, Aalto Museo, Aalto Studio Interior, Cafe Aalto, Finlandia Hall, Finlandia Hall Interior, Fiskars River Water, Forest , Helsinki Church, Helsinki Port, Kamppi Church, Kiasma,Koetalo, Lappia-talo, Olari Church, Pakila Church, Petäjävesi Old Church, Porvoo Cathedral, Rautatalo, Rovaniemi City Hall and Library, Rovaniemi Library, Säynätsalo, Sähkötalo, Tampere Cathedral, Tapiola, Tapiola Church, Tapiola Cemetery, Tapiola Hall, Tapiola Hall Top Light, Tapiola Heikintori, Turku Cathedral, Villa Mairea.

Review

寓話の表徴としての建築ディテール

Architectural Details as Signs of Fables

伏見 唯
Yui FUSHIM

本書で扱われた展覧会の展示物には、一見したところでは統一感がない。古代寺院の釘、現代住宅の障子やステンドグラス、そして近代建築のレンガ。場所、素材、作者、そして作られた時代も文脈も異なる。1つひとつの展示に惹きつけられたとしても、全体を体系的に捉えるのが難しい展覧会になっている。引率が少ないことに不安を感じるかもしれないが、むしろその全体性不在の構想こそが、これらの展覧会に込められた重要なメッセージではないかと思う。例えば何々様式の建築、何造の建築と

At first glance, the objects in this book don't have a sense of unity. They include nails from ancient temples, stained glass, Shoji, a Japanese divider with transparent sheets on a lattice frame in modern houses, and the bricks used in modern architecture. They differ in place, material, designer, and period. Even if each exhibit attracts you, systematically grasping the whole exhibition is challenging. You may feel uneasy about the lack of guidance about the exhibits' interconnection, but I think the idea of totality's absence is these exhibitions' vital message. The objects were selected so as

いった、一群の既知の形態と関連づけた印象が残らないように展示物が選ばれている (注1)。冒頭のプロローグにあるとおり、多くの地域で適用可能なデザインのメカニズムを探求しているわけだから、その共通項は形態ではない。背後の仕組みに注目している (注2)。

つまり本書に登場する展覧会は、建築デザインが生み出される前提となる集団的なメンタリティ、そしてそれが形態や空間に結実していくまでの過程といった無形の生産背景を共有するために、翻ってそのシグナルを具象に託して示そうとする挑戦的な内容である。展示物のそれぞれが物理的な美醜を放つだけでなく、いわば寓話の表徴たらんとしている (注3)。

付け足した寓話
縄と畳とバウハウス

多くの場合、デザインを生み出す仕組みは不可視であり、それは言葉や図などによって抽象的に説明されるものだ。そのため仕組みの説明が実体を正確に見せることはなく、不可視の全体性を示唆するに留まる (注4)。そこで、ある仕組みからどのようなデザインが生み出されうるのかを認識する手がかりとしては、一例を示すことが有効だ。あくまで例なので、その特殊事例そのものが伝達したいことではないが、イメージの共有に役立つ。展示物と同様にそうした仕組みを示す寓話として、3つの記事を書いた。縄 (pp42-47) と畳 (pp73-77)、そしてバウハウス (pp97-103) の話である。

縄の話では、縄文時代の竪穴住居の接合部（復元）が縄になっていることや、土器

not to convey existing architectural styles, such as Gothic and Shoin-zukuri architecture.[1] As you can see in the prologue, the common views permeating the exhibitions are not forms since it explores design mechanisms applicable in many regions. The exhibitions focus on these underlying mechanisms.[2]

The intangible background of production includes the collective mentality that is a prerequisite for creating architectural designs. The exhibition is challenging because it shows the process by which this mentality bears fruit in form or space by concretizing it. Each exhibit expresses physical beauty and ugliness but also signifies fables.[3]

Added fables: Ropes, tatami mats, and Bauhaus

In many cases, the mechanics of creating designs are intangible and described through words, diagrams, and so on. Therefore, explanations of these mechanisms do not accurately show an object's essence but suggest its intangible totality.[4] So, it's useful to give an example to convey how to create designs from a mechanism. The example is not something we want to communicate, but it's useful for sharing images. To illustrate the mechanism, I have added three fables: Ropes (pp42-47), Tatami mats (pp73-77), and Bauhaus (pp97-103).

The ropes show their role in the restored joint of a pit-dwelling house during the prehistoric Jomon period. Moreover, they exemplify how rope-patterned earthenware was both decorative and adjusted the surfaces of vessels. This exhibition asserts that "architecture made by design does not depend on its design language", paving the future of "architectural practices currently blocked by specialization". Thus, we see

の縄文が器面調整を兼ねた装飾であったことを示した。「専門化によって閉塞しつつある建築」の未来を拓くために、「建築のデザイン言語によらないデザインによって作られた建築」を目指した本展の主張の1つを、原始のものづくりに見出そうとしたのである。専門化した技術を用いずに、周囲の事物で生み出されたデザインとして。

畳の話では、建築に御簾や置畳のような舗設（しつらい）が配置されていた古代の寝殿造から、その舗設が建築にビルトインされていく近世までの流れを記した。建築は「体験する人間の側にあるもの」とし、さらに建築という分野にとらわれない「分野をまたぐ複合体」が現れるべきとする、もう1つの本展の主張にフォーカスを当てたものだ。人間の所作に対応した舗設の複合が、時の流れのなかで建築全体の生産システムに組み込まれていったことと対応させる意図である。バウハウスの話では、いかにも近代建築を象徴するバウハウス・スタイルといった白い箱のハウス・アム・ホルンと、各工房がスタイルを統一させずに協働したように見えるゾマーフェルト邸を対比した。本展の主張である「共感覚空間」に近い建築としてゾマーフェルト邸を例に挙げたかったのだ。「共感覚空間」は「オブジェクトがブロックチェーンのように連動して全体の空間領域を作り出している状態」としている。バウハウスは異分野の工房の統合を目指していて、全体に統一感のあるモダニズムらしいスタイルを進む道を選んだが、ゾマーフェルト邸のように各工房のスタイルが統一されないままに空間を構成し、異種のまま連動し合う道もありえた。その可能性に本展と通じるものがある。

primitive manufacturing as designs that things around us create without specialized technology.

The story of tatami mats describes trends from Shinden-zukuri, an ancient Japanese architecture style using movable furnishings like bamboo blinds and tatami mats, to the architecture of early-modern times, where furnishings were embedded in buildings. The story also focuses on other assertions that the exhibition makes. First, "architecture should be on the side of the person who experiences it". Second, "architecture should be complex and span many fields": The field itself should not bind it. The main point is that architecture has incorporated furnishings complexly related to human behavior into its entire production system over time.

In the Bauhaus story, Haus am Horn's white box, which symbolizes modern architecture, contrasts with the Sommerfeld House, where each studio seems to have worked together without a unified style. Sommerfeld House is a building close to *Synesthesia Scenery* that this exhibition thematizes. *Synesthesia Scenery* is defined here as "a situation that links objects like a blockchain to create an entire area". Bauhaus aimed to integrate studios in different fields and followed a modernist style with a holistic sense of unity. However, like Sommerfeld House, Bauhaus would construct a space where the studios' different styles were not unified yet co-operated. There is something in this style of architecture that parallels this exhibition.

The assertions of this exhibition enclosed in quotation marks are diverse, but they all break down the framework cultivated in the field of architecture and result in expectations that unexpected things will be mixed. The stories of ropes, tatami mats, and Bauhaus

上記の鉤括弧で括った本展の主張は多様
だが、いずれも建築分野が培ってきた枠組
みを解体し、思いもよらないもの同士が混
ざり合うことへの期待に結実するだろう。
縄と畳とバウハウスの話でも、端的に言え
ば原始から近代までの混ざり合いの歴史の
一端を示したにすぎない。

混在のリテラシー

　実際に冒頭のプロローグで示されている
これらの展覧会の行く末は、「ユニティー・
アーキテクチュア（ひとつなぎの建築）」
という理想像だ。これは「地球上の異なる
場所の異なる事柄の間に働いている無数の
因果律の全体の輪郭」だという。生産シス
テムが自ずと建築を規定する不可視の全体
性という概念を地球全体に当てはめようと
する大きな構想であり（注5）、ブルーノ・ラ
トゥールが言っているノンモダニズムの世
界像とも似ている。世界は絶えず変化する
アクターのネットワークでできていて、各
所で一時的な関係性が築かれているにすぎ
ない（注6）。世界はまず偶然性も含まれた混
沌の渦中にあり、そのなかで閉じた系の構
造が積極的に想定されてきたことは、科学
者も以前から気づいている（注7）。

　一方でクリエーションのためには、ただ
自身が混沌のなかにあることを自覚しても
仕方がない。混ざり合ったときにどのよう
な方法が効果を生むのか、そのリテラシー
を培わないとデザインを出力することはで
きないのではないか（注8）。前近代の日本に
おいても、中国から受け入れた様式を唐様
（禅宗様）と呼び、従来のものを日本様（和
様）と呼ぶなかで、それらが混ざり合った
ものを半唐様と名付けた大工家もおり（注

are, in short, a glimpse into the varied history
from primitive to modern times.

Mixed literacy

　As the prologue reveals, the these
exhibitions' main point is an ideal concept of
architecture called *Unity Architecture* (a
string of architecture). *Unity Architecture* is
defined as "the overall outline of myriad
causalities that work between different things
in different locations". One may apply the
concept of intangible totality, where
production systems naturally define
architecture, to the whole earth.[5] The idea is
similar to Bruno Latour's perspective of non-
modernism. He insists that the world
comprises a constantly changing network of
actors, and each place is built through only
temporary relationships.[6] Scientists have long
known that the world is in a chaotic whirlpool
that includes coincidences and actively
assumes closed system structures.[7]

　On the other hand, it's no use to know that
we're in chaos to create something. It is not
possible to output designs without cultivating
literacy about what methods produce specific
effects when mixed.[8] Early modern Japan
called the architectural style imported from
China *Kara-yo* (Zenshu-yo), meaning Chinese
style, and the conventional style *Nihon-yo*
(Wa-yo), Japanese style. However, some
schools of carpenters called a mixture of
these styles *Han-Karayo*,[9] a quasi-Chinese
style, meaning that two styles were mixed
with a certain degree of regularity. However,
if the style becomes a mere façade, it
becomes a fixed form and loses the tension
between two different things. The combined
style of architecture that originated in the
medieval period is clearly superior to the
earlier one. In other words, the style cannot
be vibrant unless it constantly changes, but it

9)、混ざり方にある程度の法則性をもって
いたと思われる。ただし形骸化すれば1
つの固定化された様式になり、異種が混ざ
り合う緊張感は次第に失われていくことだ
ろう。中世に生まれた折衷様の建築は、初
期のものが明らかに優れている。つまり絶
えず変化していかないと活きてはこない
が、そのことも含めた混在のリテラシーの
醸成。

　これらの展覧会で展示されている建築の
ディテールの数々は、そうした混在のリテ
ラシーを説明するための寓話の表徴にちが
いない。混沌の世界では、純粋な閉じた系
は常に外圧にさらされている。その外圧を
受け入れること、そして自身が世界の混沌
のなかにいると認めることが受動的な態度
であり、さらに混沌の渦中にあってもそこ
で生きていくためのリテラシーを見出して
いく。それが、本書主題「受動的能動性」
ではないか。

also contributes to the development of
literacy for mixing styles.

　The architectural details in these
exhibitions must signify fables to explain the
literacy of such a mixture. In a chaotic world,
a pure closed system is constantly under
pressure. Accepting external pressure and
acknowledging that you are in the world's
chaos is a receptive attitude and a way to
find the literacy to live amidst the chaos. They
lead to this book's theme: *Receptive
Activism*.

■注釈

注1 筆者は展覧会の企画には関与していない。ただし、執筆依頼を受けた段階で渡邊大志氏に「未来の建築を考えようとしているので、既存の建築のなかに本展の意図に完全に沿ったものは見出せない」と聞いた。そのため、あえて建築の全体像を示さず、意図に近い要素の集積で理念の全体をおぼろげに炙り出そうとしている。

注2 このあたりに注目する建築観は、建築の上部構造（様式）と下部構造（生産構造）の「連関」に注目した中川武『木割の研究』（博士論文、1985年）に通じるものがある。渡邊大志氏の関心は建築生産史研究の延長にあるように思える。

注3 寓話は地域を超えて共感されやすい。例えば古代ギリシャの寓話はアジアでも時には教訓となる。本展の展示物は日本のものだが、地域を超えた共感を目指しているという点で寓話の表徴のようなものではないか。

注4 「不可視の全体性」は前掲『木割の研究』の言葉である。標準寸法、規格材などの仕組みの導入により、建築は「ものの形式としての実体的な全体性」から「不可視の全体性」への経路を歩み始めたとする。

注5 注4参照。

注6 久保明教『ブルーノ・ラトゥールの取説 アクターネットワーク論から存在容態探究へ』、月曜社、2019年。

注7 I.プリゴジン、I.スタンジェール『混沌からの秩序』、みすず書房、1987年。

注8 大江宏『建築作法 混在併存の思想から』（思潮社、1989年）に「たんなる無秩序の混在併存ではだめなんだ（中略）それぞれの相関性を与えるなんらかのシステムが発見されなければならない」とある。

注9 『建仁寺派家伝書』や『林家木割書』（いずれも東京都立中央図書館特別文庫室）に見られる。

■ NOTES

1 I was not involved in the planning of the exhibition. However, I referred to the words of Taishi WATANABE, the exhibition supervisor: "I'm trying to think about the architecture of the future, so I don't perfectly align the purpose of this exhibition with any existing historical context of architecture". Therefore, I intentionally did not show the whole image of the architecture but obscured this idea by accumulating elements close to the intention.

2 This architectural perspective is similar to a 1985 doctoral thesis by Takeshi NAKAGAWA, *Kiwari no Kenkyu*, which focuses on the linkage between architecture's superstructure (style) and the substructure (production structure). The supervisor's interest seems to lie beyond the study of architectural production history.

3 Fables are relatable across regions. Ancient Greek fables, for example, can be instructive even in Asia. Although the exhibits in this exhibition are from Japan, they signify fables by aiming for relevance across regions.

4 *Kiwari no Kenkyu* mentions the term "intangible totality". With the introduction of proportional member sizes, materials with standard sizes, and other mechanisms, architecture has begun to follow a path from a "substantive totality as a form of thing" to "intangible totality".

5 Ibid.

6 Akinori Kubo, *Bruno Latour no Torisetsu Actor–network theory kara Sonzaiyotaitankyu he* (Tokyo: Getsuyosha, 2019).

7 Ilya Prigogine and Isabelle Stengers, *Order Out of Chaos* (Japanese edition), (Tokyo: Misuzu Shobo, 1987).

8 Oe Hiroshi, *Kenchiku Saho Kontonheizon no Shiso kara* (Tokyo: Shichosha, (1989). "We can't just have a mixture of disorder... we have to find some system that gives us a correlation".

9 *Kenninjiha kadensho* and *Hayashike kiwarisho* (Both are stored in the Special Collection Room of Tokyo Metropolitan Central Library).

伏見 唯 （ふしみ・ゆい）

建築史家、編集者。1982年東京都生まれ。早稲田大学大学院修士課程修了後、新建築社、同大学院博士後期課程を経て、2014年伏見編集室を設立。『TOTO通信』などの編集制作を手掛ける。博士（工学）。

Yui FUSHIMI

Architectural historian and editor.
Born in Tokyo in 1982. He began his career at Shinkenchiku-sha Co. Ltd., a publishing company dedicated to architecture. He then established Fushimi & Editors Co., Ltd. in 2014. He worked on the editing and production of TOTO Tsushin (TOTO 通信), an architectural magazine.
Ph.D. (Architecture) from Waseda University, Tokyo, Japan

Epilogue

新たな普遍（ポスト・コロナ）のなかの
Unity Architecture
Unity Architecture in the New Universal（Post COVID-19）

　本書に収録されたフィンランドとドイツでの3つの展覧会及びそれらに関連するテキスト群は、私がフィンランドで暮らしていた2020年の春にお披露目する予定でした。そして、在日本フィンランド大使館での展覧会はそれらを1つにまとめた帰国展という位置づけでした。しかしながら、未曾有の世界的パンデミックによって外国での展覧会は1年以上の延期となり、帰国展であったはずの東京での展覧会も出国展となってしまいました。

　逆に言えば、未知のウイルスによって人

The three exhibitions in Finland and Germany, alongside a collection of related texts, would be scheduled for the spring of 2020 (while I was still living in Finland). Additionally, the exhibition planned for the Embassy of Finland in Tokyo, Japan, had always been envisioned as a homecoming exhibition that would conceptually pull all three together. However, due to the unprecedented global pandemic, which also hit in the spring of 2020, the Finnish and German exhibitions were postponed for more than a year. Furthermore, the exhibition in Tokyo—which was originally the

間にはどうすることもできない状況とシナリオが描かれたとも言えます。私はそれを受け入れることから全てを始め直さねばなりませんでした。

パンデミックによって帰国展から出国展へと正反対の文脈に位置づけ直されたため、本書はこれから行う各国での展覧会のためのカタログの後に製作されました。つまり東京を含めた3か国・4都市の異なる文脈から同一の展示物について記述した書物と展覧会の間には、時系列の「ねじれ」が生じてしまったわけです。

しかし、これこそが未知のウイルスによる攻撃という人類史上でも有数の外圧を受け入れつつ、自らの表現に昇華する、という私がフィンランドでの滞在中に思い至ったナショナル・ロマンティシズムのメカニズムをまさに実践していたのだと思うのです。おそらくは多くの人たちもそれぞれのタスクについて同じようなことが起きていることでしょう。

そのように考えてみれば、これからの社会はコロナウイルスのような外圧の受容をいかに表現に変換するのかといった視点から考えられていくことが重要になってくるでしょう。

本書はナショナル・ロマンティシズムを第3の場所に拓く方法を発見し、言葉では言い表せないと思われてきた(あるいは、言語化できないために近代的ではないと思われてきた)デザインや建築が「美しく在る」ということが、いかに人間社会において必要不可欠な論理であってきたのかを示そうとするものです。

パンデミックによる度重なる延期は、フィンランドに身を置きながら思考した3

homecoming exhibition—was actually held before the other three exhibitions. Notably, the impact of the pandemic-induced postponement turned what would have been a "homecoming" exhibit into a "departure" exhibit.

In other words, the reality that there are situations and scenarios beyond our control was revealed by an enigmatic virus. The first thing I had to do was to start all over again by accepting that reality.

The book was produced after the catalogues for the upcoming international exhibitions in Finland and Germany, just as the pandemic repositioned Tokyo's exhibition in the exact opposite context from being the homecoming exhibition to being the departure exhibition. In other words, "twists and turns" of time arose between the exhibitions and this book, which describes the same exhibit from the different contexts (i.e., three different countries and four cities, including Tokyo).

However, this seems to me to be exactly the same mechanism of national romanticism that I had come to grasp while living in Finland. Namely, that I could sublimate the pressure into my own expressions, while simultaneously experiencing (and learning to accept) one of the greatest external pressures in human history: the COVID-19 pandemic. Presumably, many people had experienced a similar situation in the midst of their own, unique conditions.

If we think about it in this way, then it will also be important to consider how, in the future, society can positively transform the reception of external pressure (like those arising from the COVID-19 pandemic) into its own expression.

On this note, this book aims to discover

つの展覧会とカタログの考えを、日本という外から眺める視点を持つ機会をもたらしてくれました。そしてそのことは、Nation of Sorrow の場所における Crossover-Architecture による Synesthesia Scenery な空間の実践、という流れ全体の呼称を考えるために私には十分な時間でした。その行為のなかには、一度ウイルスという外圧によって折られた計画（プラン）を立て直す際のかすかな美の存在があり、その美は計画を描き直すための論理そのものでした。

　こうしてささやかながら私もまた、外から自分を観ることで他者に観てきたものを自身に観ることができたのです。本書のタイトルとした Unity Architecture という概念は、フィンランドに渡る以前から模索し続けていたものでした。しかし、渡フィン以前はまだ漠然としたものであり、その証拠にこの対訳となる上手い日本語が思い付けずにいたのです。外国での自分の考えを母国で再検討するという機会は、「ひとつなぎの建築」という対訳を私に思いつかせました。

　言語は、言葉の意味以上に言葉の意味が持つ性質の創造に大きく関わるものです。

　フィンランドの人々と話していると、しばしば Sisu（シス）と彼らが呼ぶ精神的なスタミナを表す概念に触れることがあります。強大な外圧にどれだけ圧迫されてもなお、折れない心のようなものです。それは単にたくましいというプリミティブな精神を言っているのではありません。継続的に抑圧された心理状態にぎりぎりのところで耐えながら、その水面下ではしっかりとした自己の根を張ることを怠らない、まさ

ways in which we can open up national romanticism to expand into a third space, and thereby show the beauty of design and architecture—something which has often been considered ineffable (or, for some, considered not to be modern because of its non-linguistic nature)—as an indispensable logic in society.

　Nonetheless, the postponements resulting from the pandemic have provided the opportunity to review the ideas foundational to the three exhibitions and each of their catalogues. I was also able to do that during my stay in Finland, and to do so from an outside perspective. Furthermore, the postponements gave me enough time to think about the naming of the overall flow weaving through each of the three exhibitions' themes. The main current of thought is the practice of Synesthesia Scenery (the theme of the Weimar venue) by the theory of Crossover-Architecture (the theme of the Berlin venue) in the field of Nation of Sorrow (the theme of the Helsinki venue). Furthermore, within the interconnected themes, I saw a faint beauty while reconstructing the plan that had been broken by the external pressures caused by the virus. The beauty was the logic itself, which fueled the reasons for redrafting the plan.

　In this way, I was also able to see what I saw in others in myself. I gained access to this insight by looking in from the outside. I had already explored the concept of Unity Architecture before I had moved to Finland. However, before I went to Helsinki, the English concept was still vague in my own mind, and I actually could not yet properly express the concept in Japanese—my own, native language. The opportunity to reconsider what I had been thinking about

にロマンティシズムの境地のようなメカニズムがSisuにはあると、彼らにとって外国人である私にも感じることができました。もちろん、そこにはフィンランドと日本の人々の伝統的な民族意識のなかで共通する部分があったことも大きかったのでしょう。それは一説にはフィンランド語が日本語と同じウラル・アルタイ語族に分類されるということからも分かるような気がします。

こうした同種のものからやがては異種のものも含めて、それらはそれらのままで互いにリンクしていく「ひとつなぎの建築」（Unity Architecture）は、外圧を受け入れることから始めねばならないポストコロナの時代に最も尊い建築の姿のような気がしてなりません。これから、少しずつ多くの人たちと一緒に「ひとつなぎの建築」の一部を私も作っていきたいと思います。

2021年7月末
渡邊大志

when I had been abroad, once I was back in my own country again and communicating daily in my own native language, made me think of "a string of architecture" as a Japanese translation for Unity Architecture.

What this experience helped me realize, is that language has so much to do with how the meaning of words is actually created beyond their dictionary definitions.

When I talk to Finnish people, I often come across the concept of Sisu, by which they mean "spiritual stamina". Sisu is like a heart that won't break—no matter how much pressure it gets from the outside. It's not just a spirit of primal strength. As a foreigner, I also felt that Sisu has a mechanism similar to the state of romanticism, which also endures a state of continuous oppression until the very end. It never fails to take firm root under the surface. Of course, one of the main reasons I felt this way is that there is a commonality between the traditional nationalism of the Finnish people and that of the Japanese. Another reason could also be that the Finnish language could be classified as part of the Ural-Altaic language family, which also includes the Japanese language.

"Unity Architecture"—which means "A String of Architecture" in Japanese—includes many things and links them together just as they are. This seems to be the most important approach to architecture in the post-COVID-19 era—an era in which we must begin architecture by accepting external pressures. In the future, I would like to build a part of Unity Architecture with even more people involved.

End of July 2021
Taishi WATANABE

Profile

渡邊大志 （わたなべ・たいし）

1980 年生まれ。早稲田大学創造理工学部建築学科准教授。

2005 年、早稲田大学理工学術院建築学専攻修了（石山修武研究室）。同年、石山修武研究室個人助手。

2012 年、東京大学大学院工学系研究科博士課程修了（伊藤毅研究室）。博士（工学）、一級建築士。

2016 年より現職。専門は、建築デザイン・都市史。

2019 年から 2020 年まで、フィンランド・アアルト大学客員研究員。

株式会社渡邊大志研究室一級建築士事務所主宰、世田谷まちなか観光交流協会委員、港区景観審議会委員、第 22 期日本建築学会代議員。

主な作品・展覧会に、「節会 ―倉庫と舞台―」、「レッドハウス」、「モリスハウス・シリーズ」、「ブルーインフラがつくる都市」展、「空気のグロッタ」など。主著に、『東京臨海論―海からみた都市構造史―』（東京大学出版会、2017）など。受賞歴に、東京建築士会住宅建築賞金賞 (2021)、日本フィンランドデザイン協会賞 (日本フィンランドデザイン協会、2021) など。

Taishi WATANABE

Born in 1980. Associate professor at the architecture department of Waseda University.

In 2005, he graduated from the department of architecture of the Graduate School of Creative Science in Waseda University (Osamu Ishiyama Lab), and served as a personal assistant to Osamu Ishiyama Lab.

In 2012, he graduated from the doctoral program of Graduate School of Engineering in Tokyo University (Takeshi Ito Lab). He became a doctor of Engineering and a licensed architect in Japan.

From 2019 to 2020, he had been a visiting researcher in Aalto University, Finland.

He is the founder of Taishi Watanabe Laboratory Architectural Office, the committee member of Setagaya Tourism Exchange Association, the committee member of Minato-ku scenery council, and the 22nd delegate of Architectural Institute of Japan.

Notable works and exhibitions:
"Sechie - Stage and Strage -", "Red House", "Morris House Series" "Blue Infrastructure Making the City exhibition", "Air Grotta - Hiding Information -", etc.

Writings:
"Tokyo's Coastline: A History of the Urban Structure Formed by the Distribution of Warehouses on the Port of Tokyo" (University of Tokyo Press, 2017), etc.
Awards:
Gold Prize in Residential Architecture Prize (Tokyo Society of Architects & Building Engineers, 2021), JFDA Award (Japan Finland Design Association, 2021), etc.

ひとつなぎの建築
― 3つのプロジェクト・3つの展覧会・18のオブジェクト ―

初版：2021 年 10 月 4 日発行
編著：渡邊大志

協賛：スカンジナビア・ニッポン ササカワ財団
制作協力：アアルト大学、ベルリン工科大学、
　　　　　バウハウス大学ワイマール校、フィンランド大使館、
　　　　　在フィンランド日本大使館、渡邊大志研究室
展覧会後援：在フィンランド日本大使館、在ドイツ日本大使館、
　　　　　　フィンランド大使館、フィンランドセンター
翻訳（本文）：牧忠峰
アートディレクション：新昭彦
エディトリアルディレクション：倉西幹雄
発行所：株式会社 ADP
　　　　〒165-0024 東京都中野区松が丘 2-14-12
　　　　Tel. 03-5942-6011
　　　　Fax.03-5942-6015
印刷・製本：廣瀬印刷
©2021 Taishi WATANABE, Yrjö SOTAMAA, Pentti KAREOJA,
Jörg H. GLEITER, Verena VON BECKERATH, Yui FUSHIMI
Printed in Japan
ISBN978-4-903348-55-1 C3052
禁無断転載

Unity Architecture
― 3 Projects, 3 Exhibitions, 18 Objects ―

Date of Publishing : First Edition October 2021
Edited and Written by Taishi WATANABE

Sponsor : Scandinavia-Japan Sasakawa Foundation
Production Cooperation : Aalto University, Technische Universität Berlin,
　　　　　　　　　　　　Bauhaus-Universität Weimar,
　　　　　　　　　　　　Embassy of Finland in Japan,
　　　　　　　　　　　　Japanese Embassy in Finland,
　　　　　　　　　　　　Taishi WATANABE Laboratory
Exhibitions Support : Japanese Embassy in Finland,
　　　　　　　　　　　JapaneseEmbassy in Germany,
　　　　　　　　　　　Embassy of Finland in Japan,
　　　　　　　　　　　Finnish Institute in Japan
Translation (Main Texts) : Tadamine MAKI
Art Direction : Akihiko ATARASHI
Editorial Direction : Mikio KURANISHI
Published by ADP Company　https://ad-publish.com
Printed by Hirose printing., in Japan
©2021 Taishi WATANABE, Yrjö SOTAMAA, Pentti KAREOJA,
Jörg H. GLEITER, Verena VON BECKERATH, Yui FUSHIMI
ISBN978-4-903348-55-1 C3052
All rights reserved